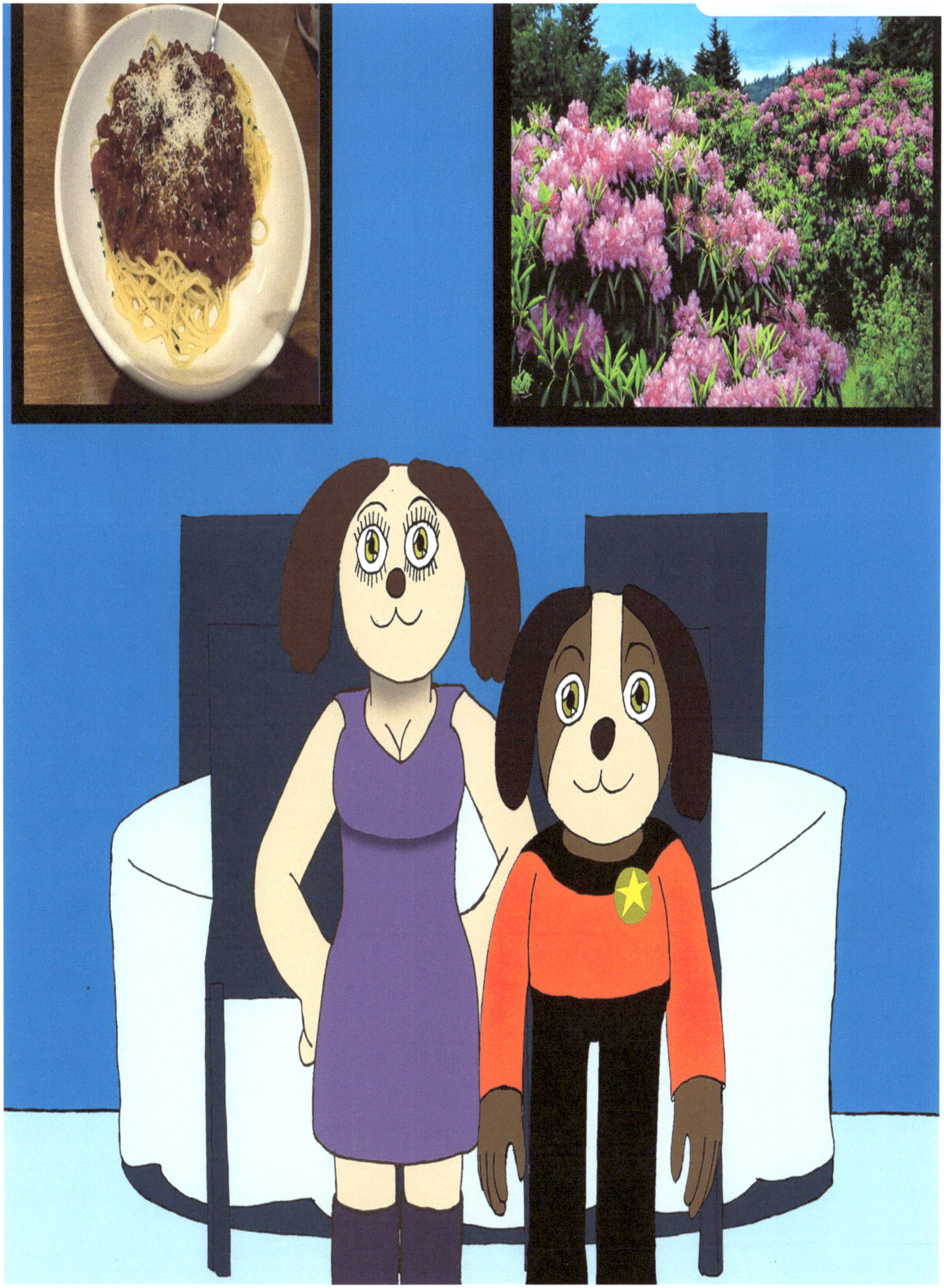

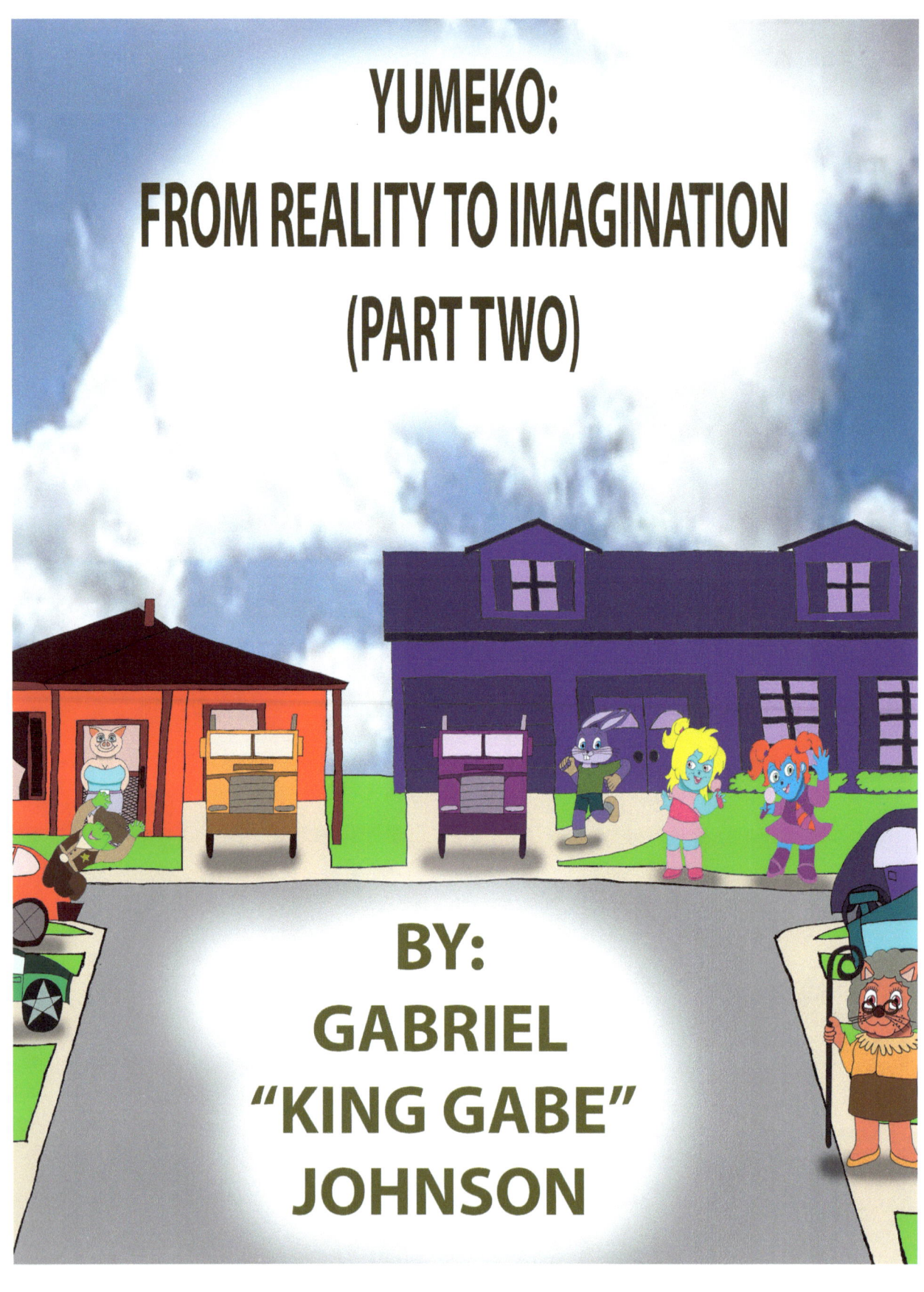

This is a work of fiction. The events and characters described herein are imaginary and are not intended to refer to specific places or living persons. The opinions expressed in this manuscript are solely the opinions of the author and do not represent the opinions or thoughts of the publisher. The author has represented and warranted full ownership and/or legal right to publish all the materials in this book.

YUMEKO #2
FROM REALITY TO IMAGINATION (PART TWO)

All Rights Reserved
Copyright © 2023 Gabriel "King Gabe" Johnson

Cover artwork and images © 2023
Gabriel "King Gabe" Johnson
and Christina "Queen Tina" Johnson

This book may not be reproduced, transmitted, or stored in whole or in part by any means, including graphic, electronic, or mechanical without the express written consent of the publisher except in the case of brief quotations embodied in critical articles and reviews.

PRINTED IN THE UNITED STATES OF AMERICA

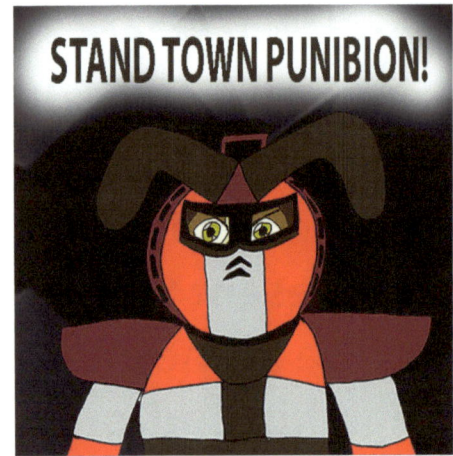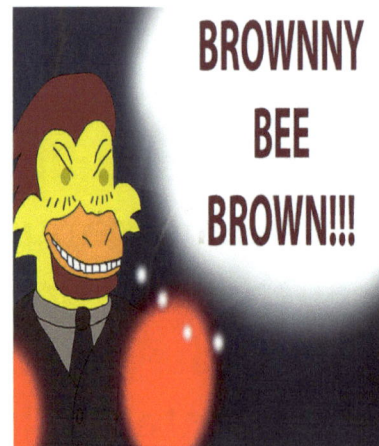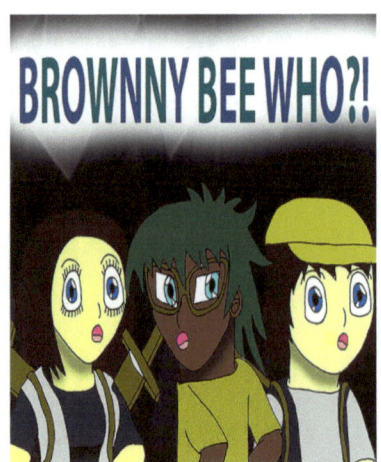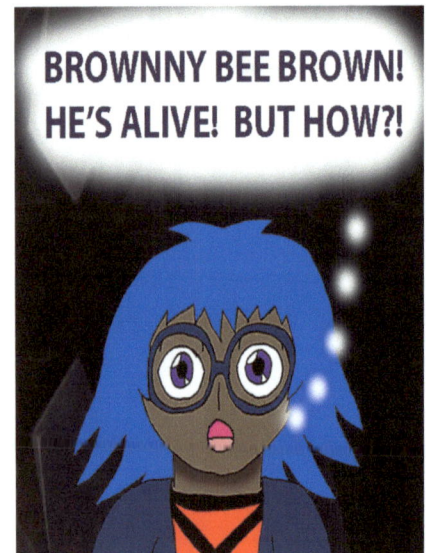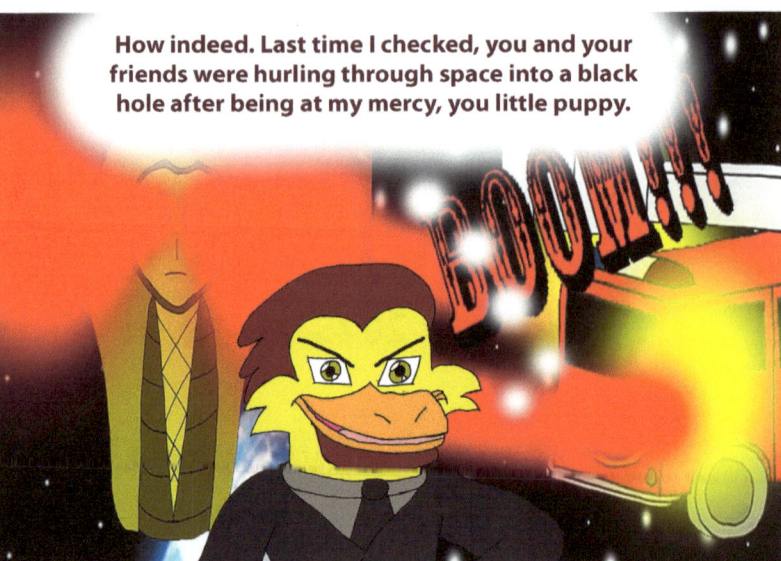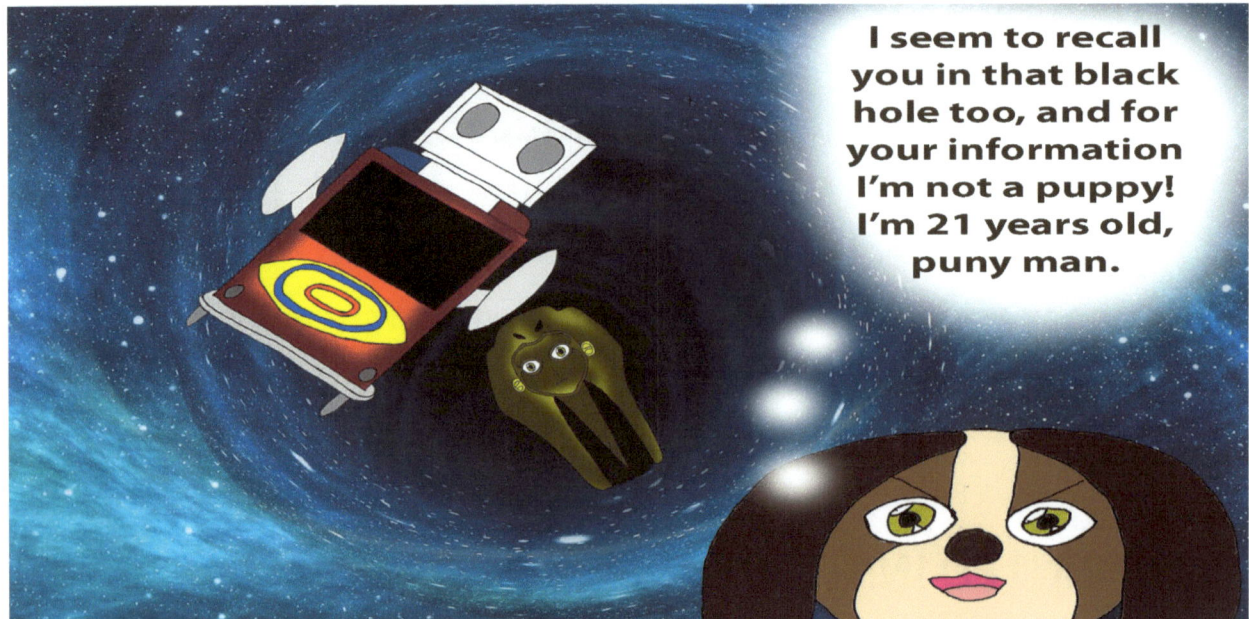

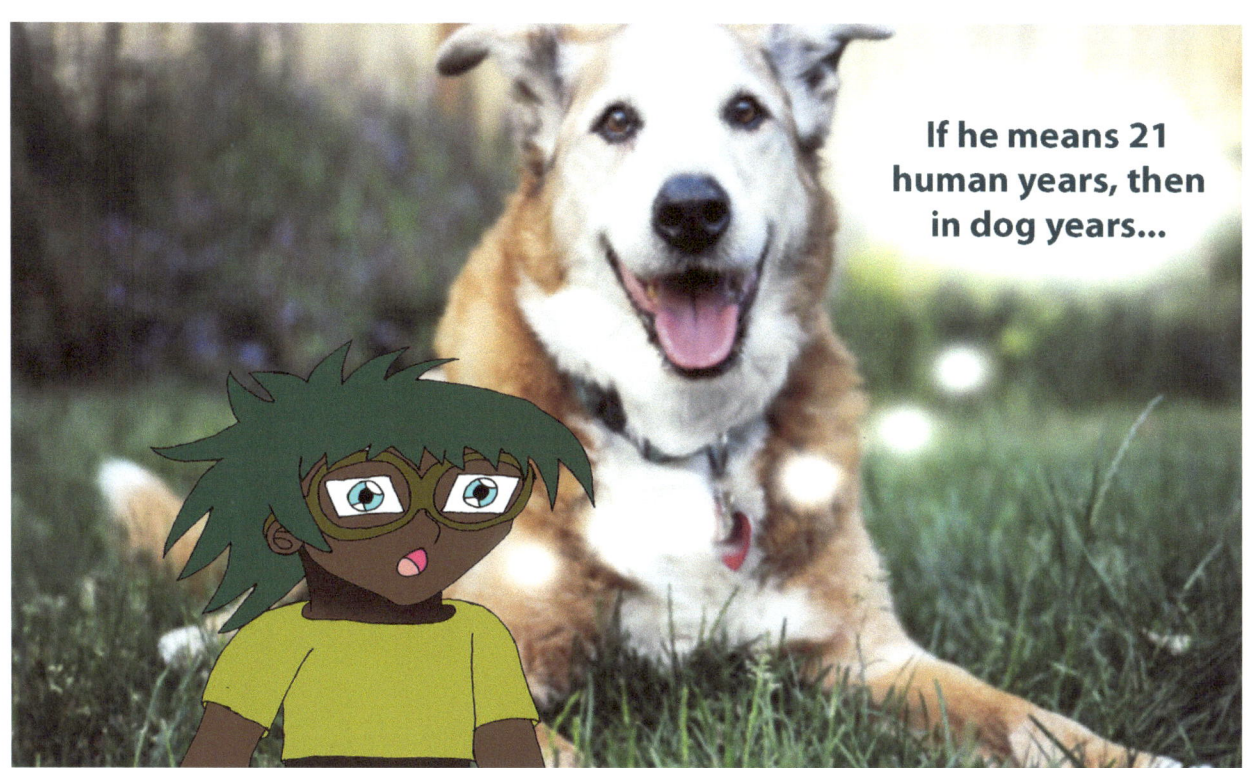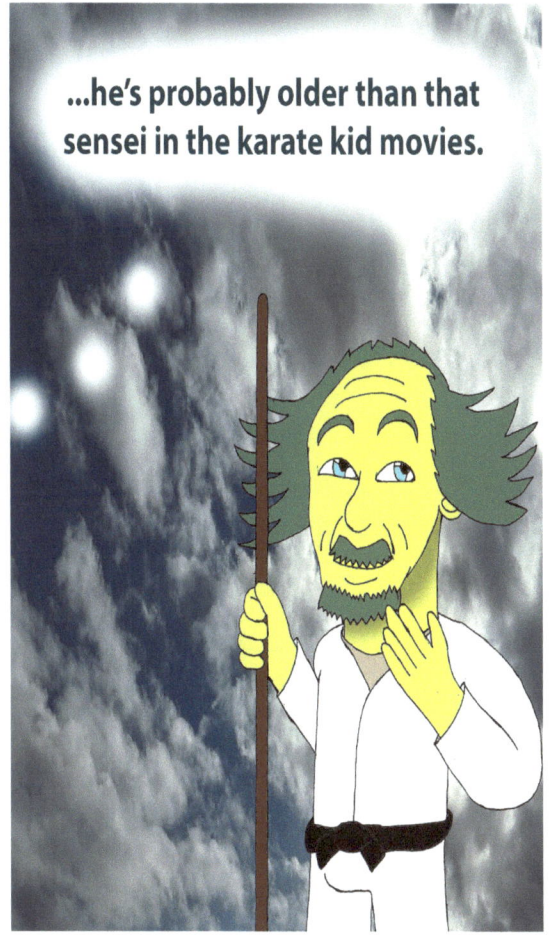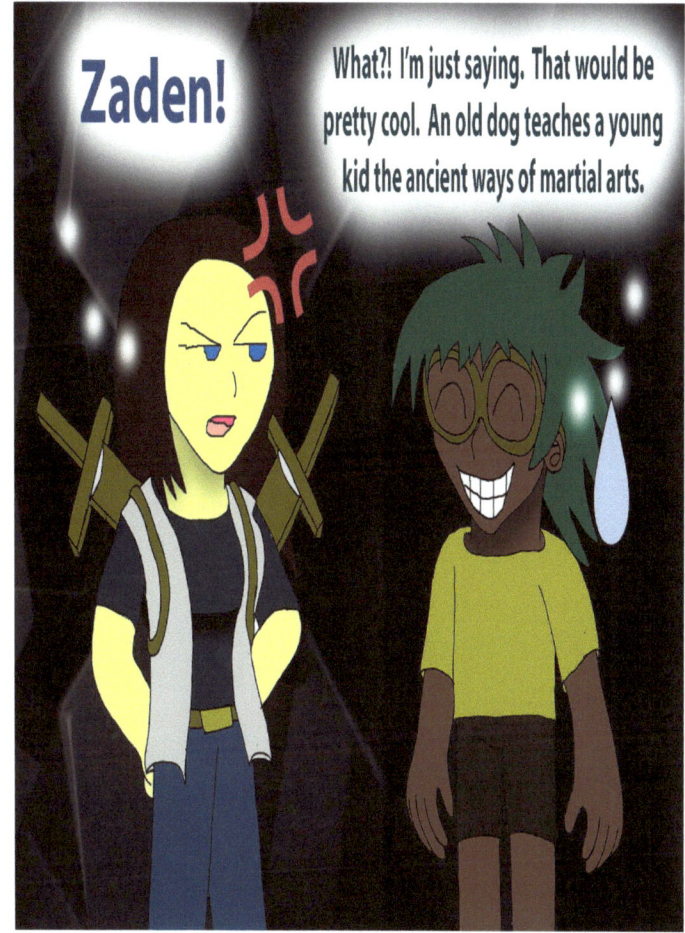

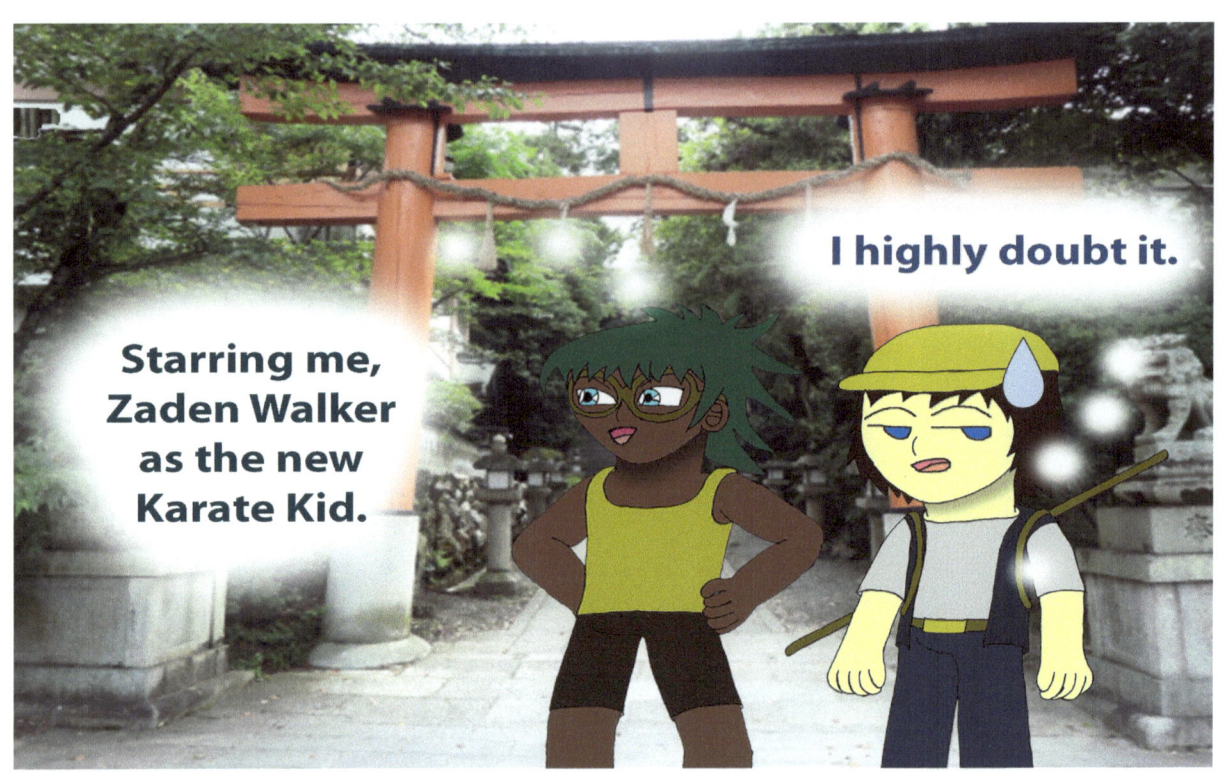
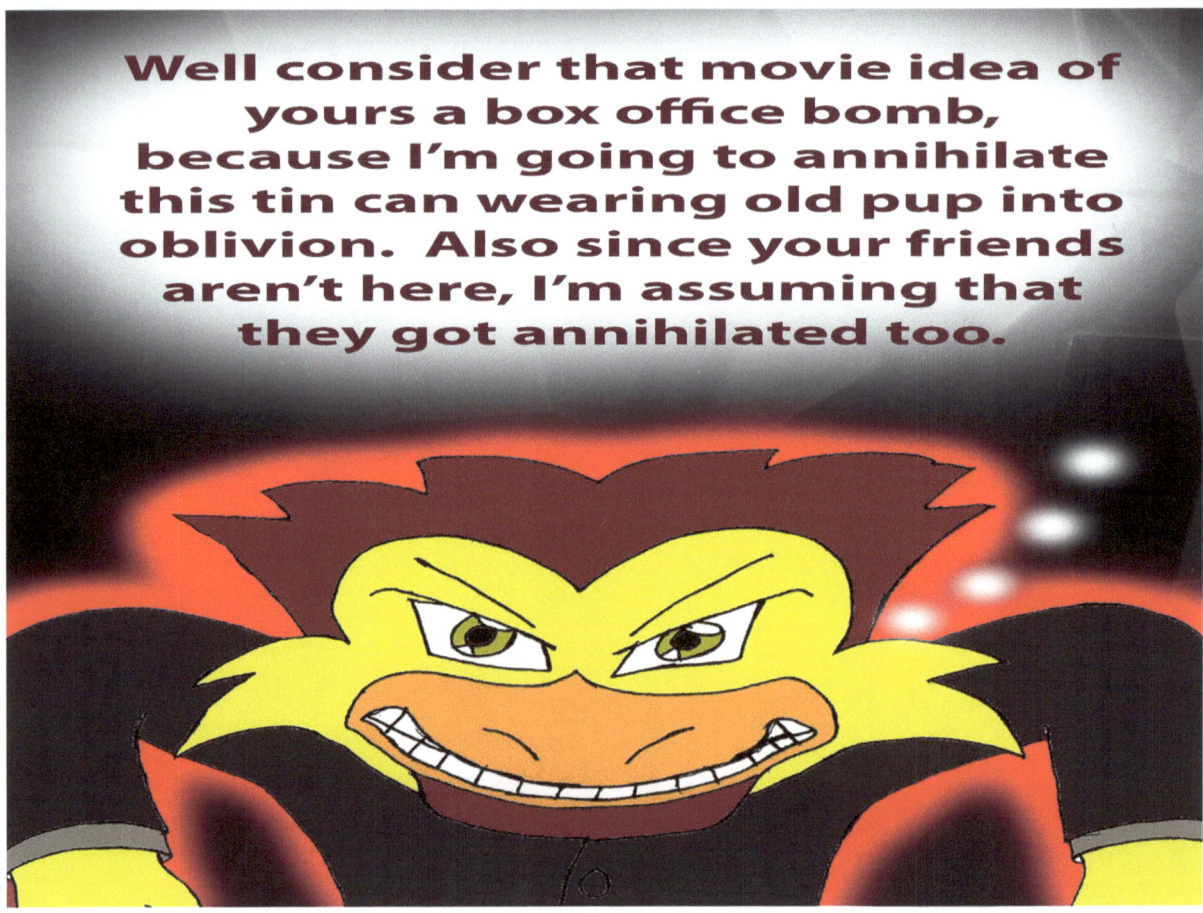

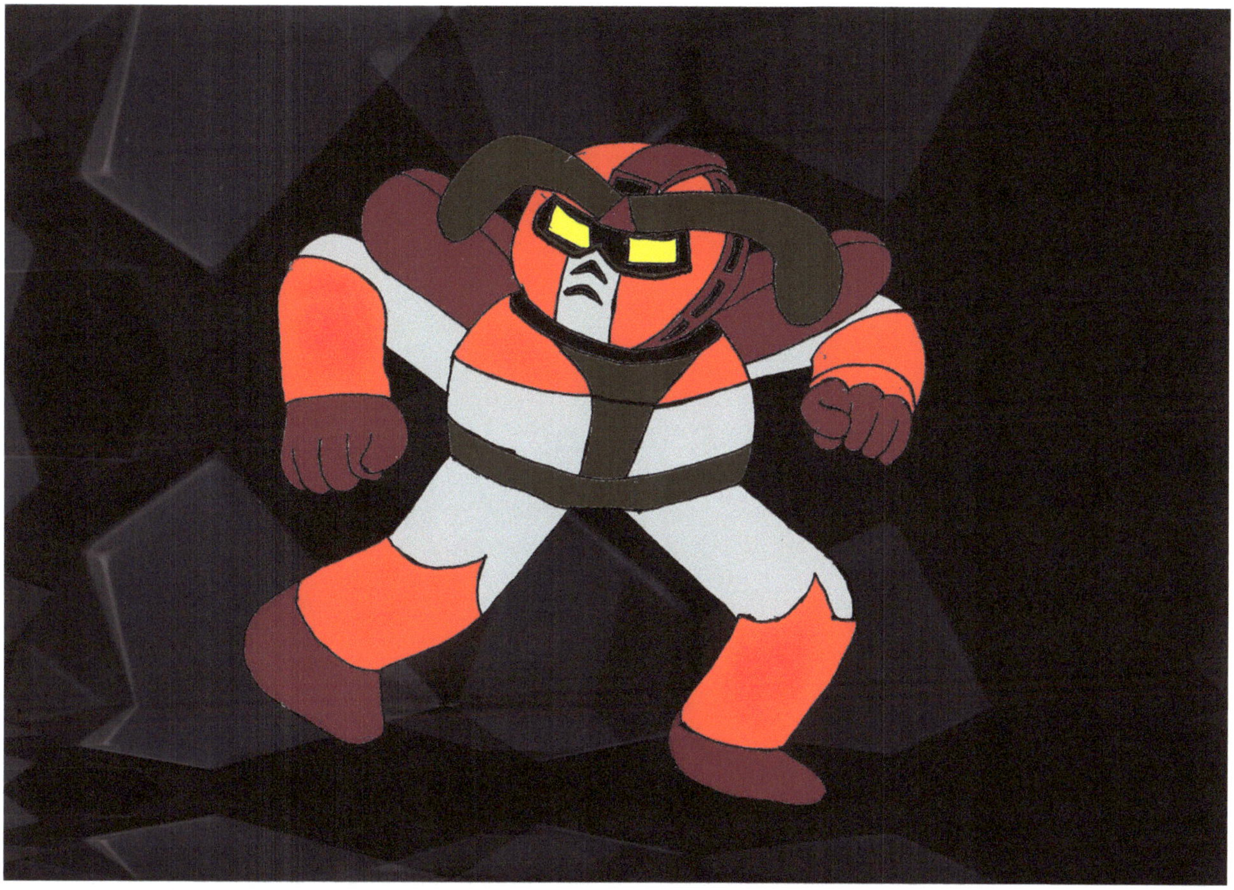

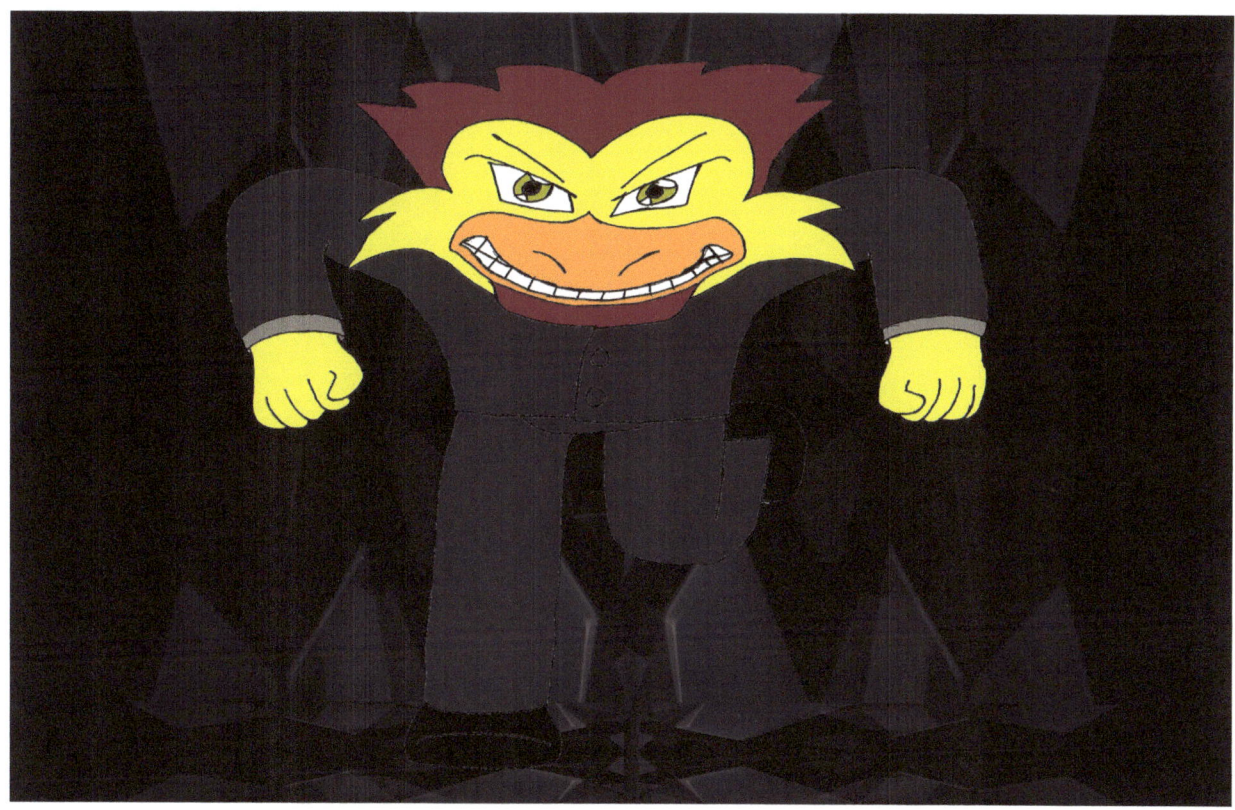

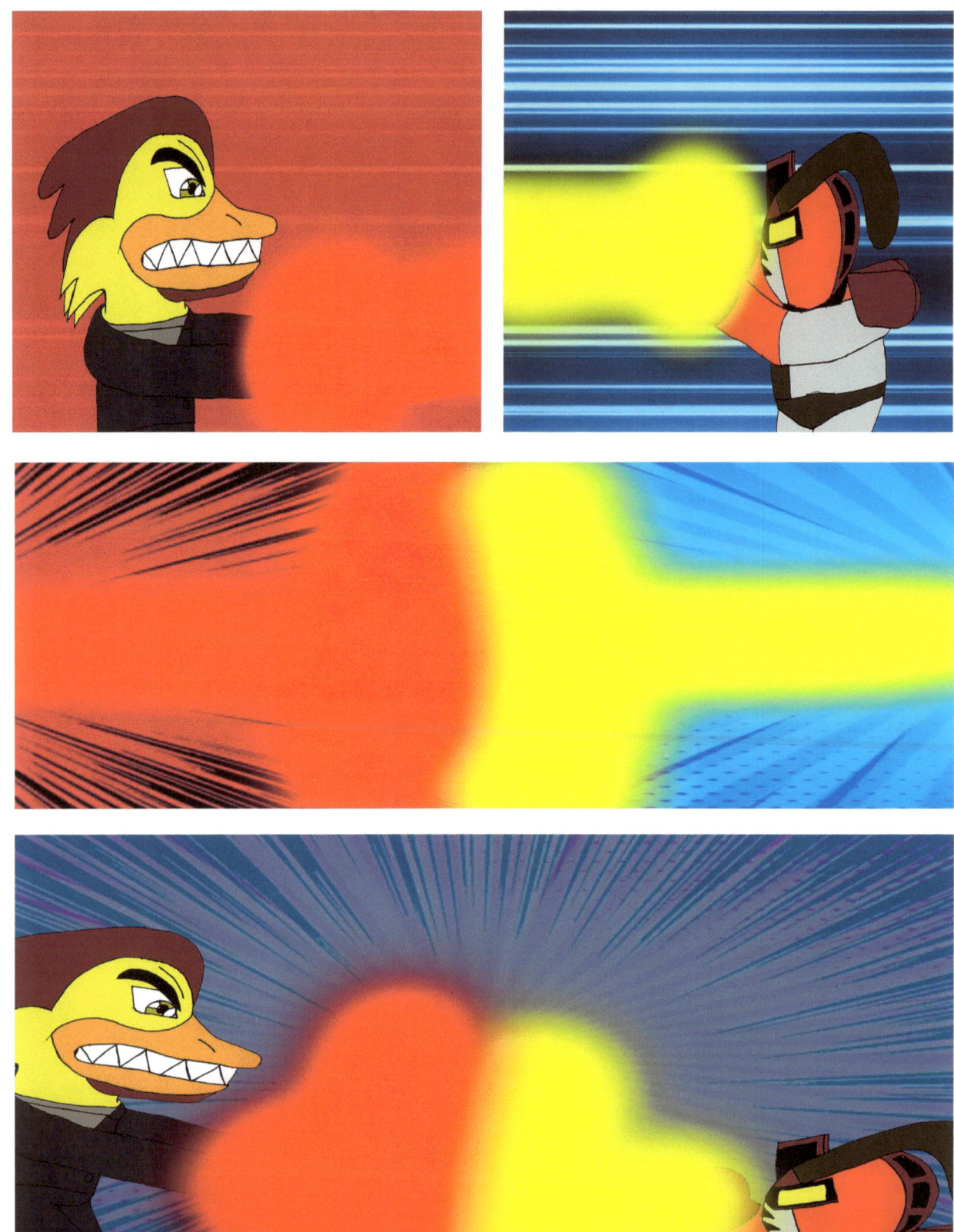

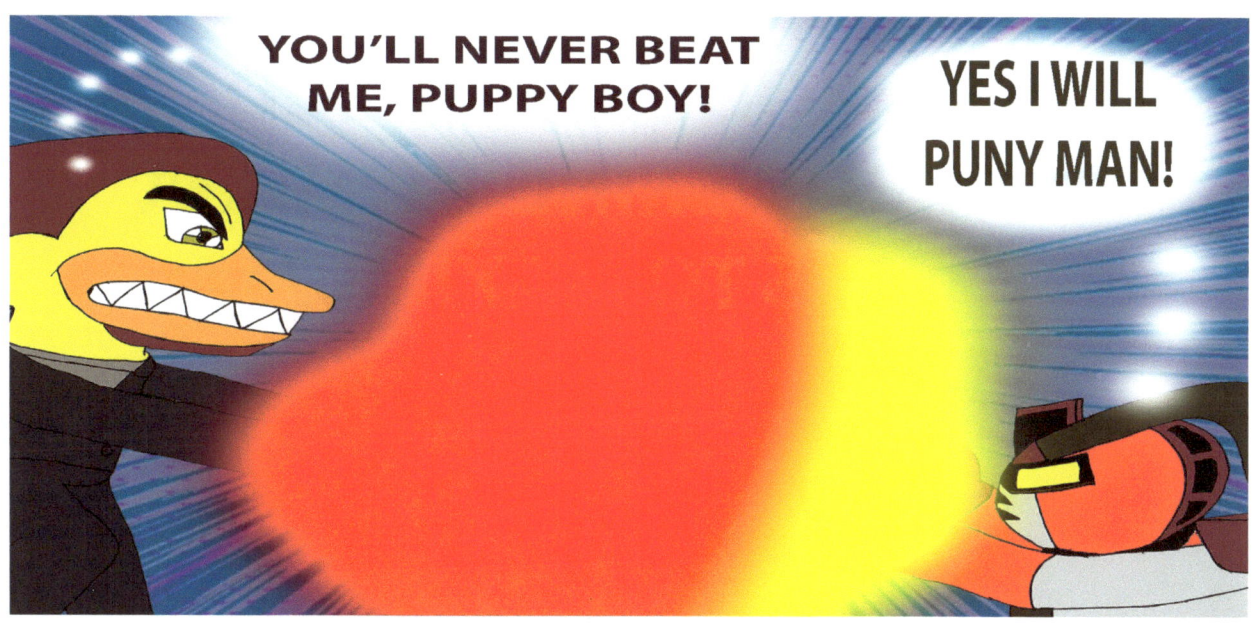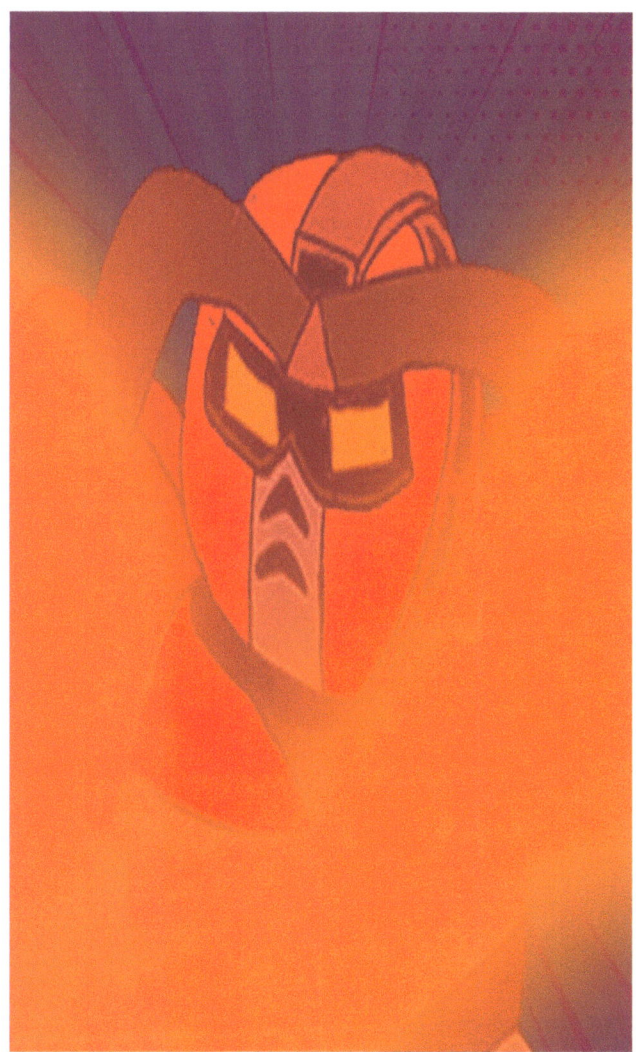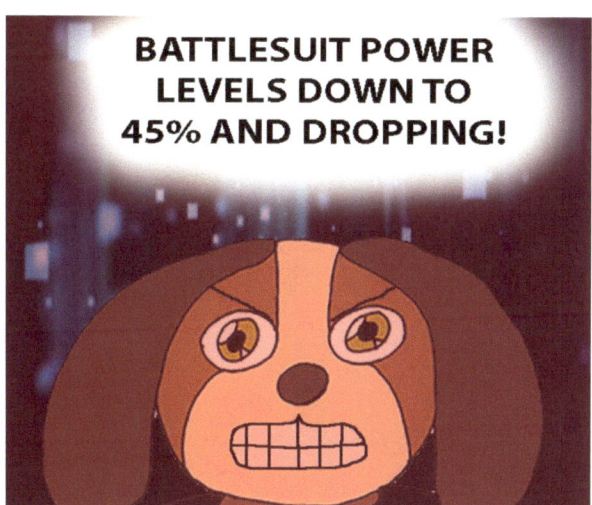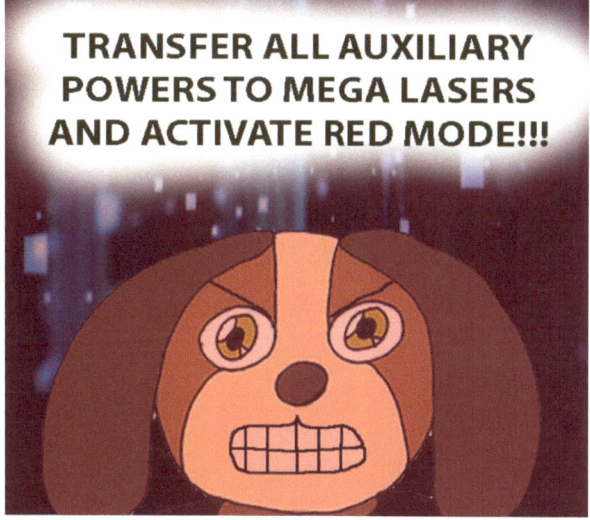

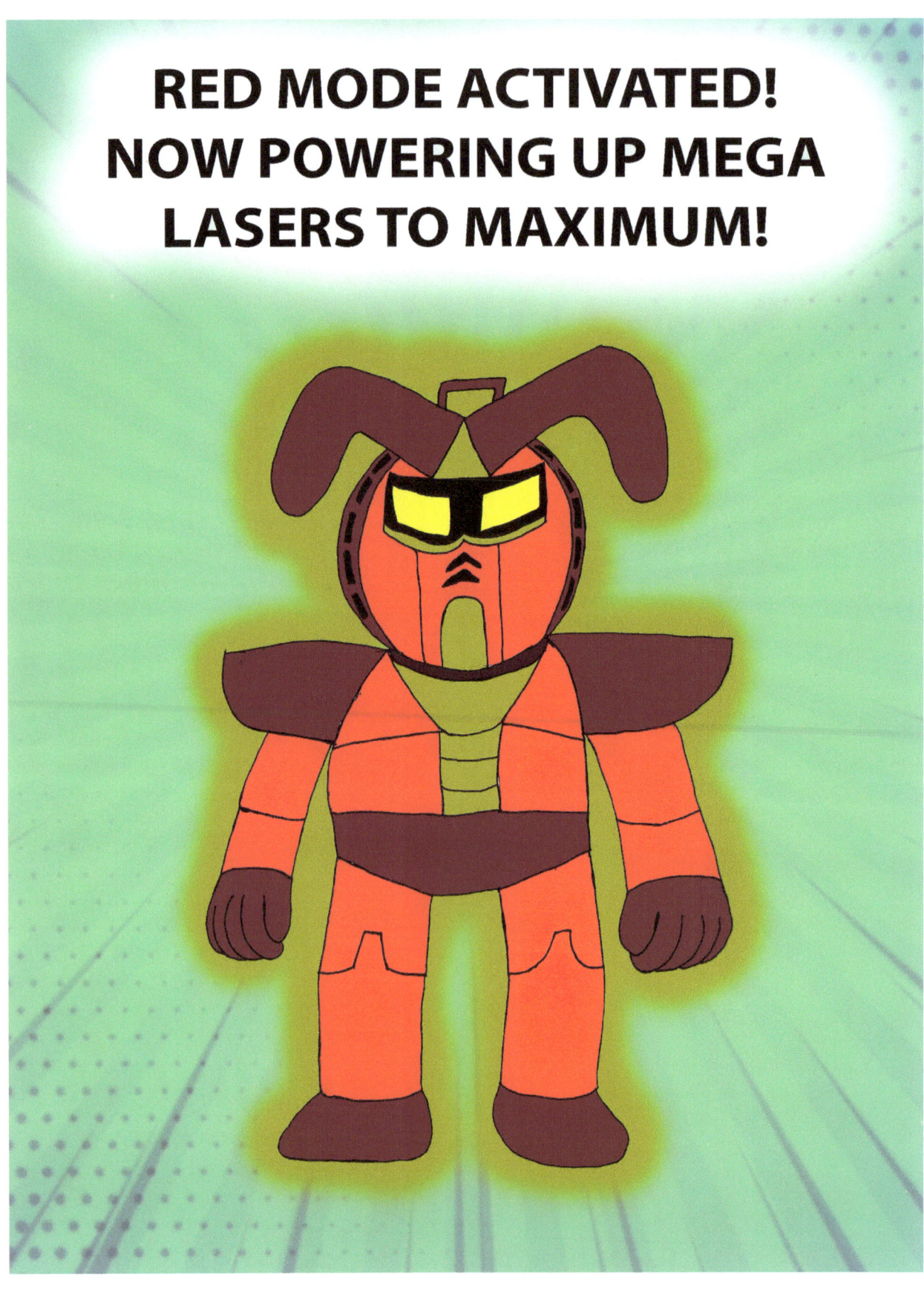

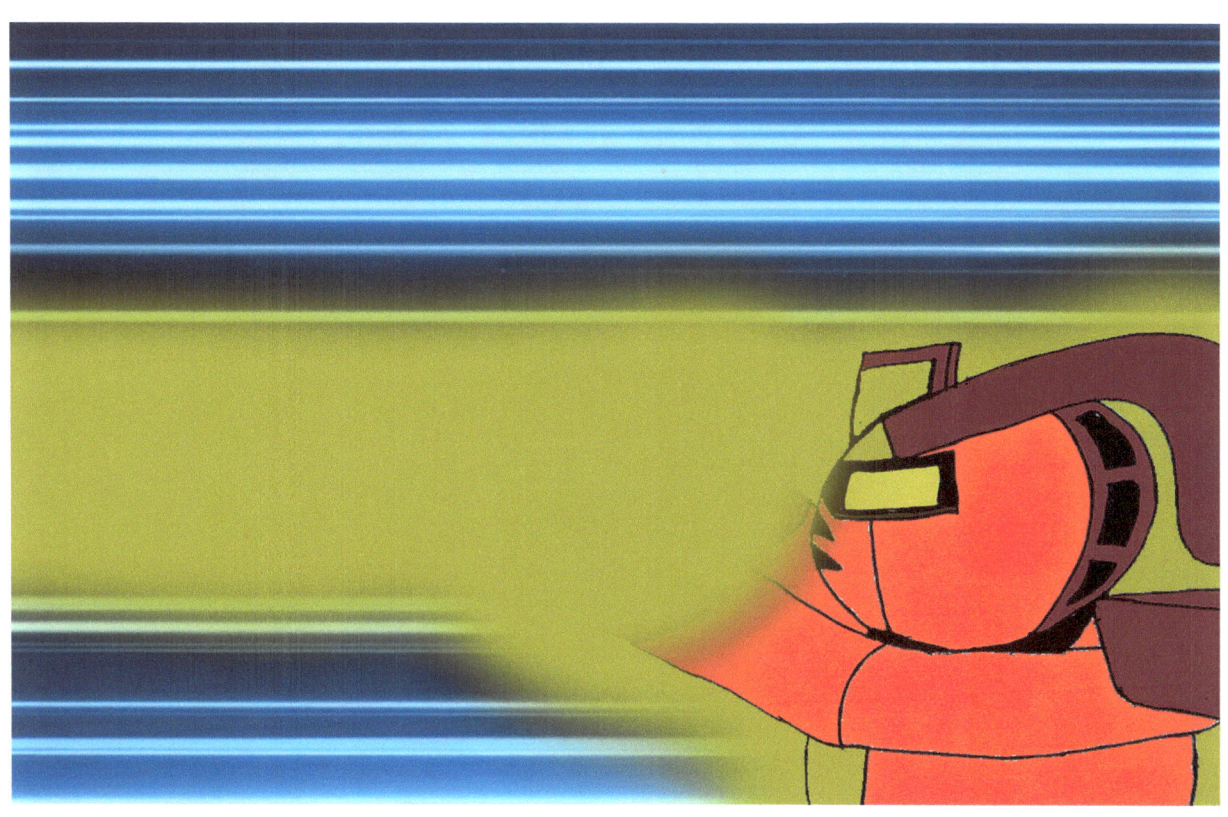
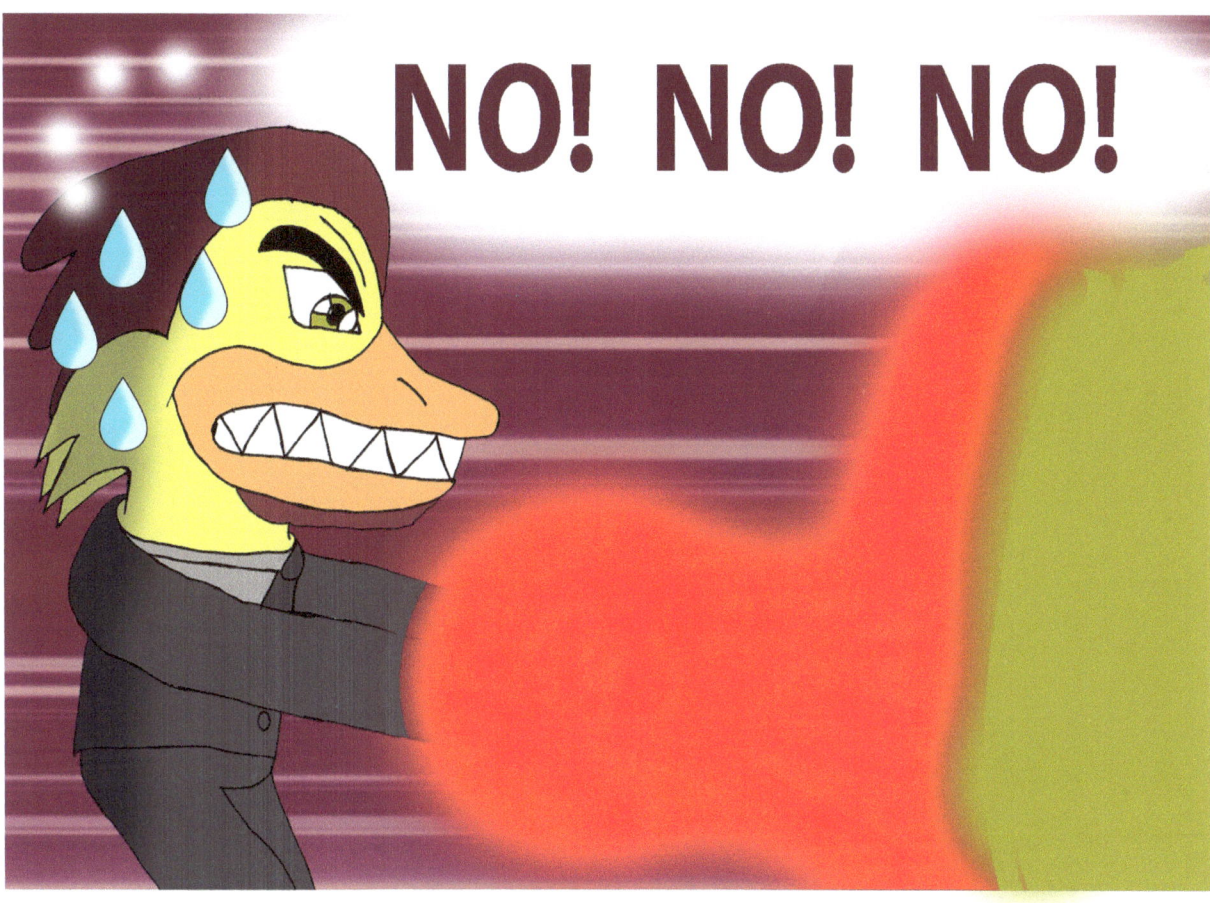

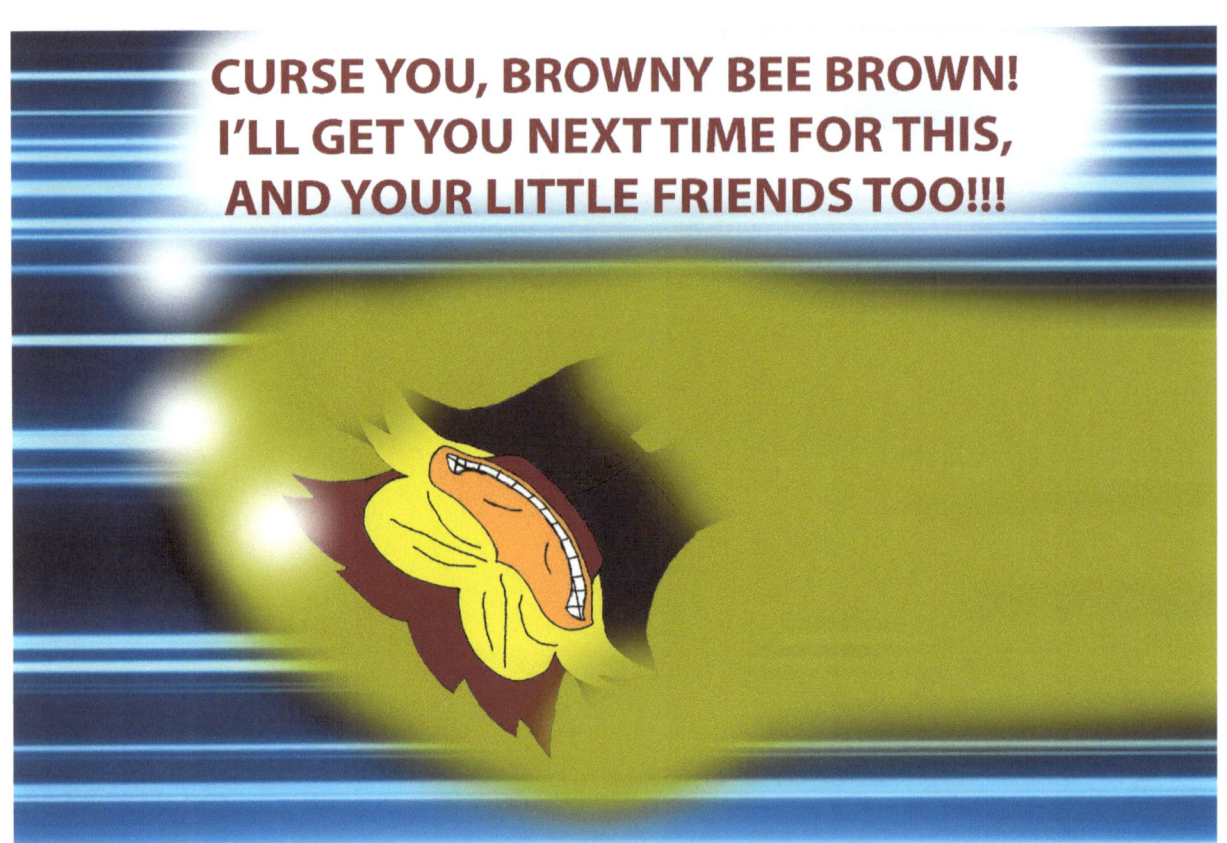
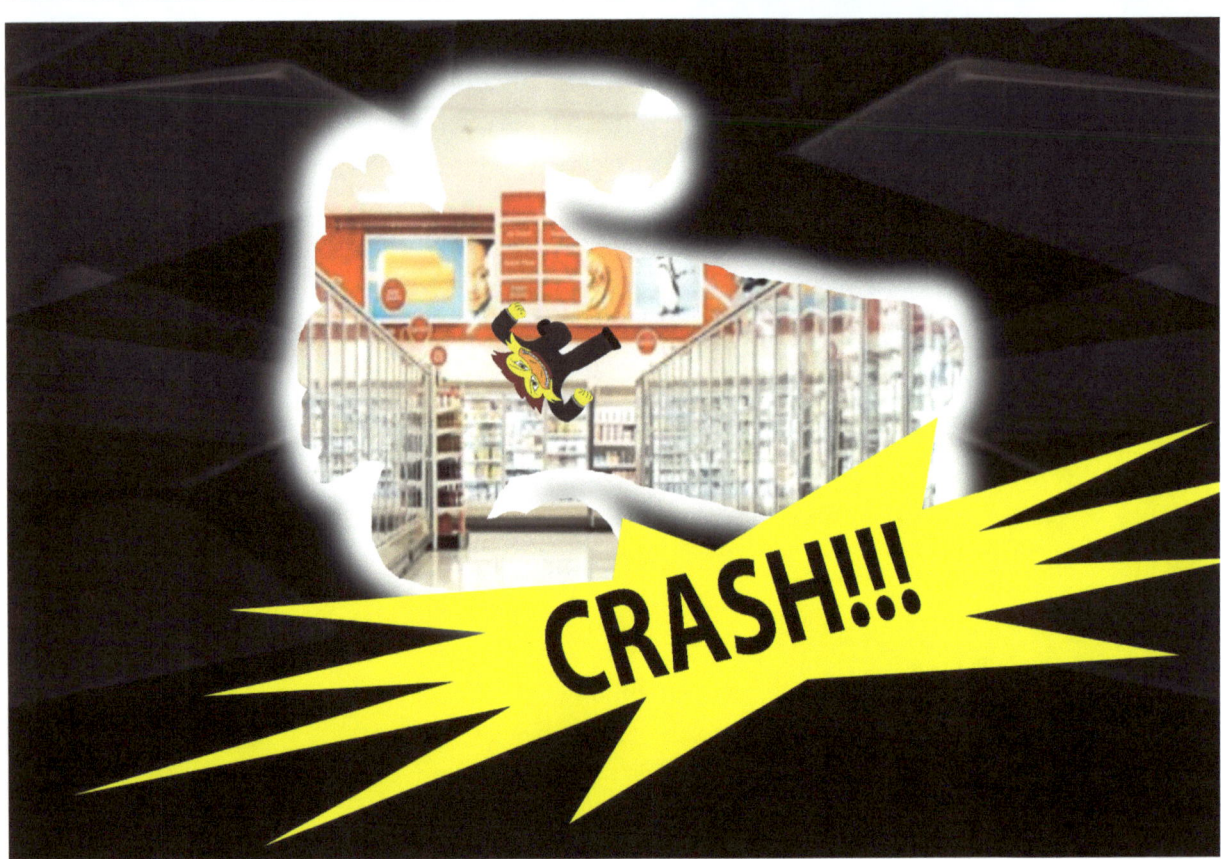

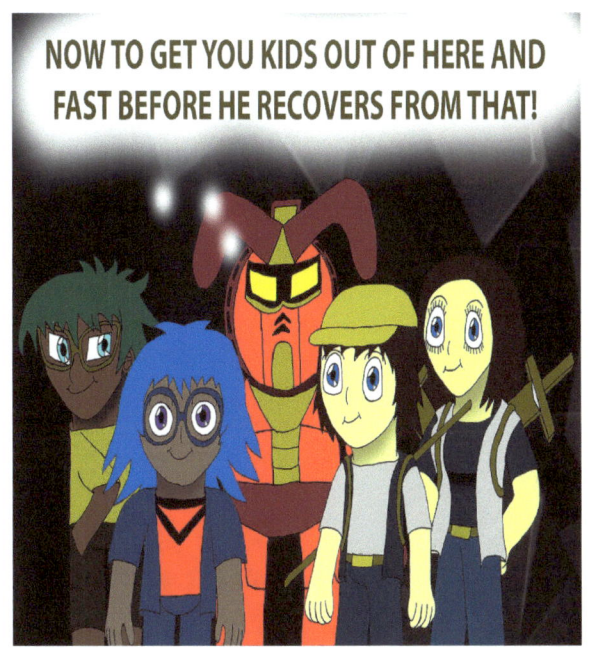
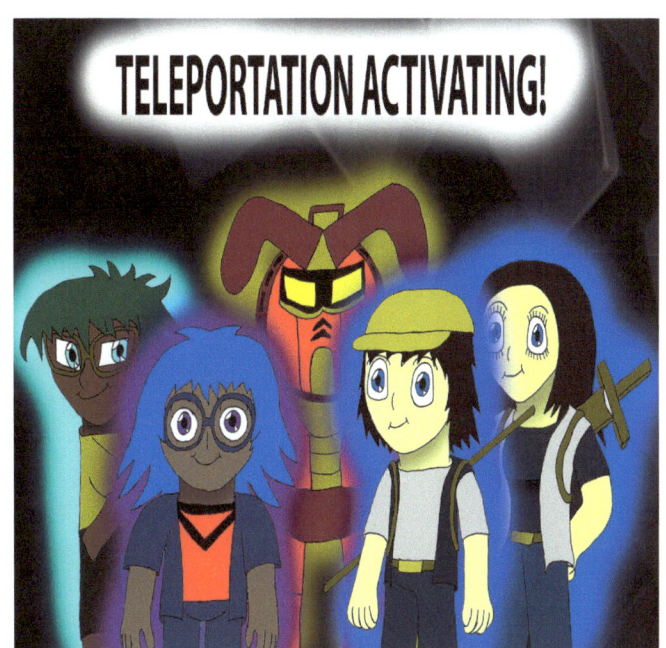
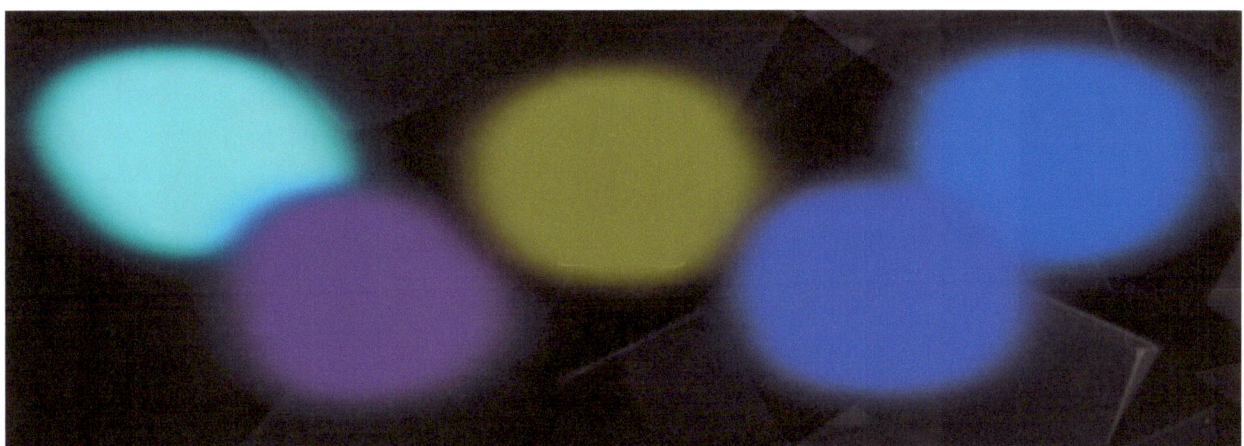
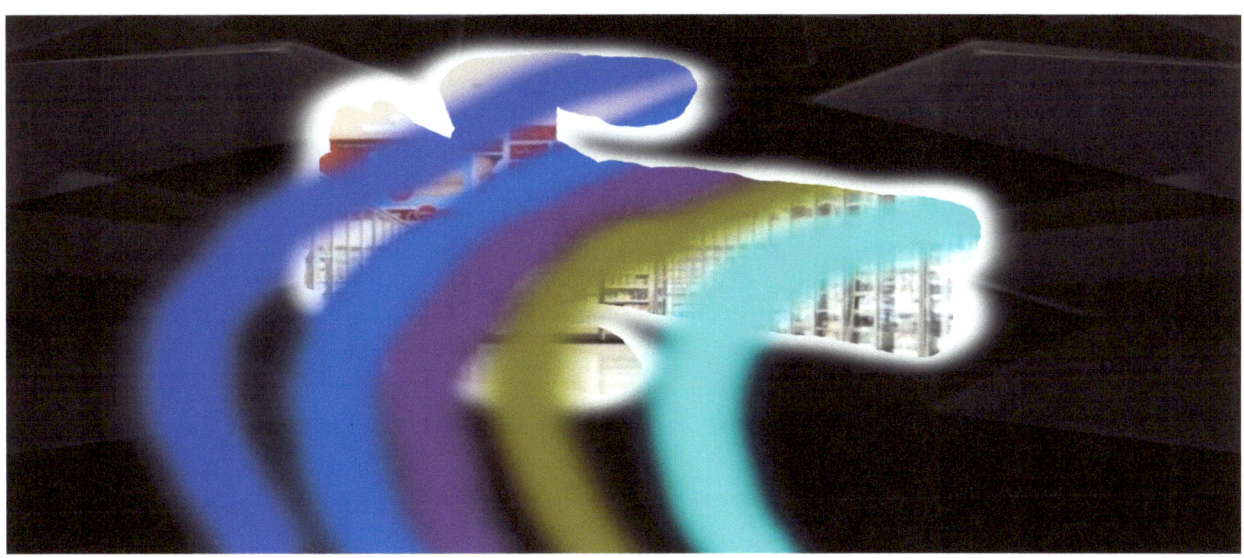

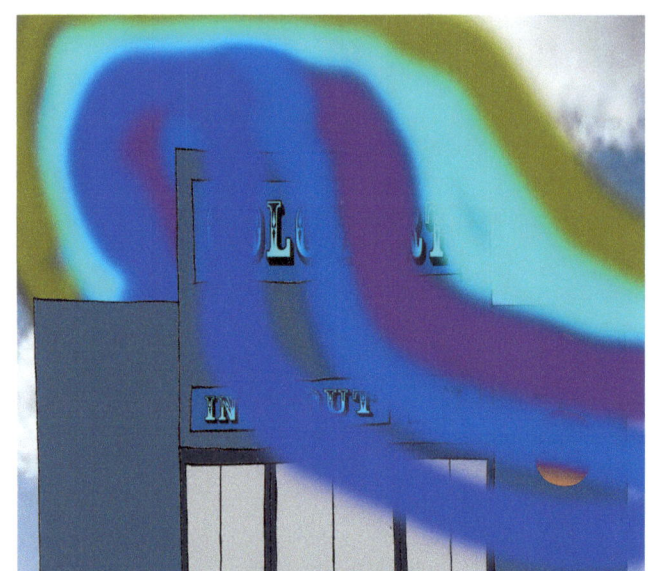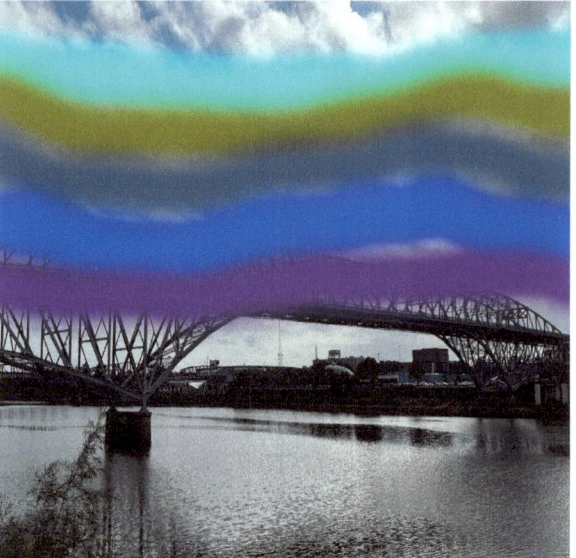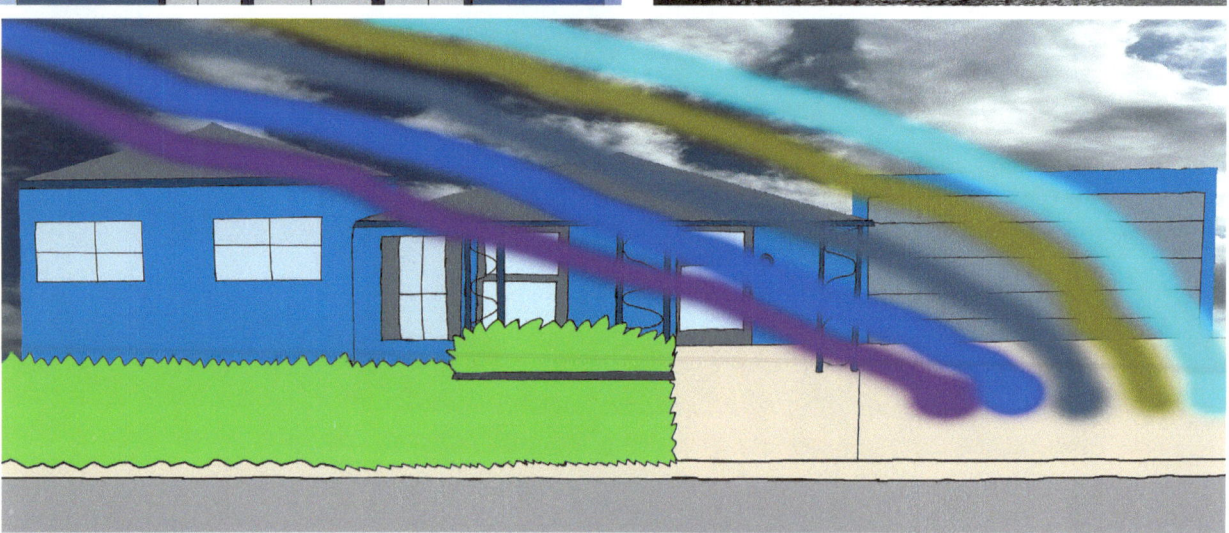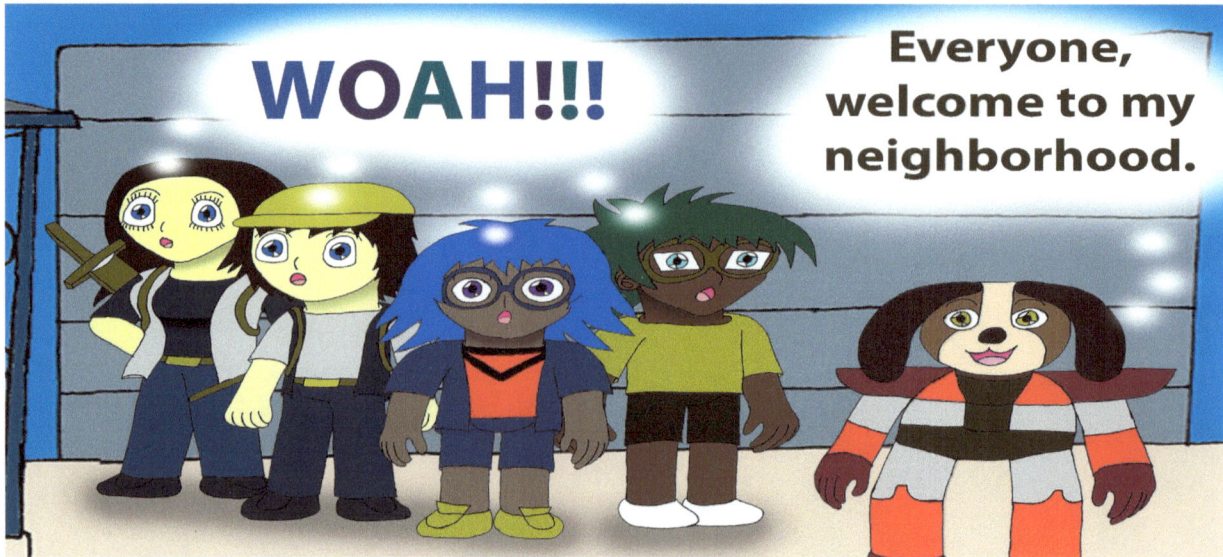

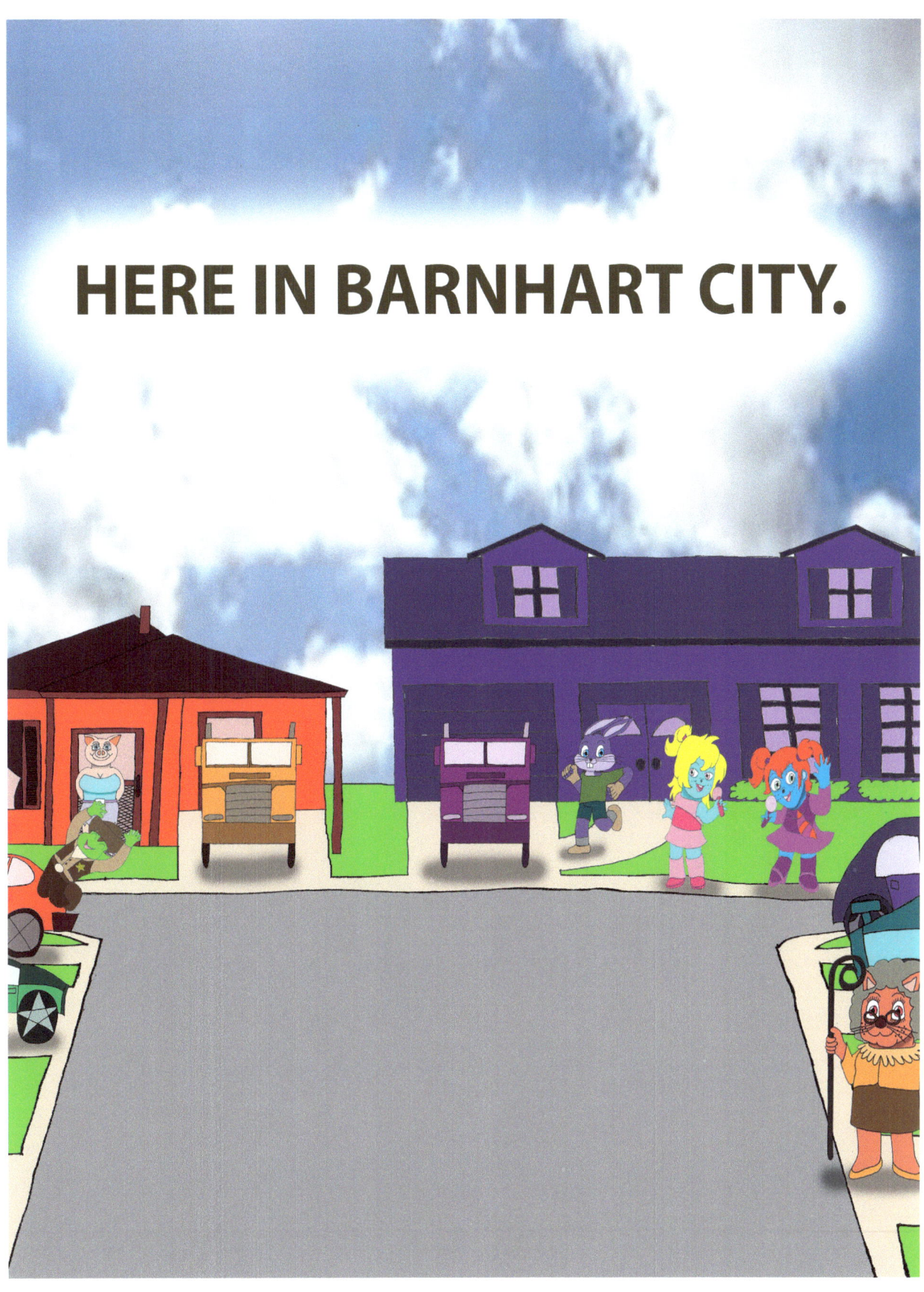

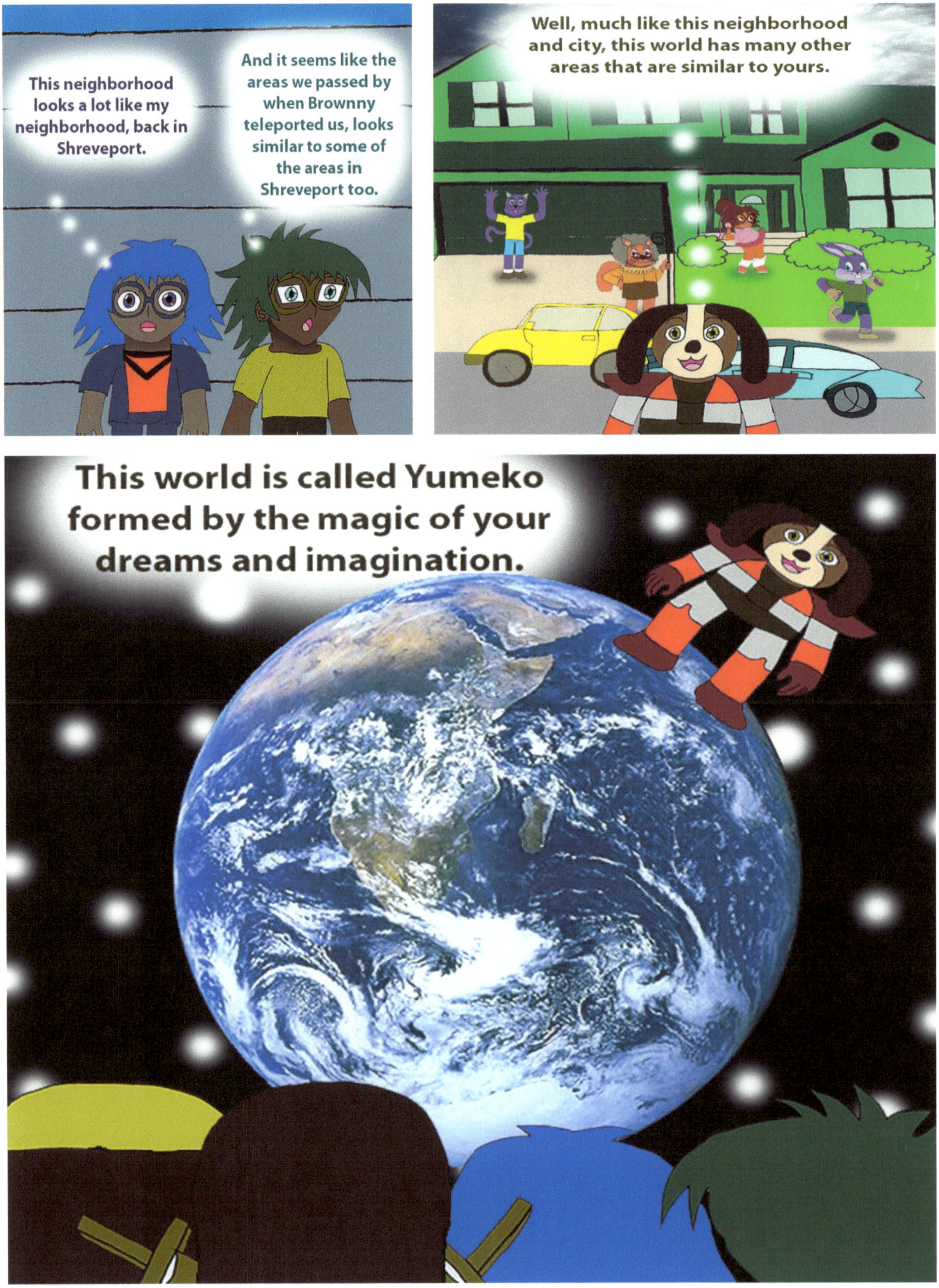

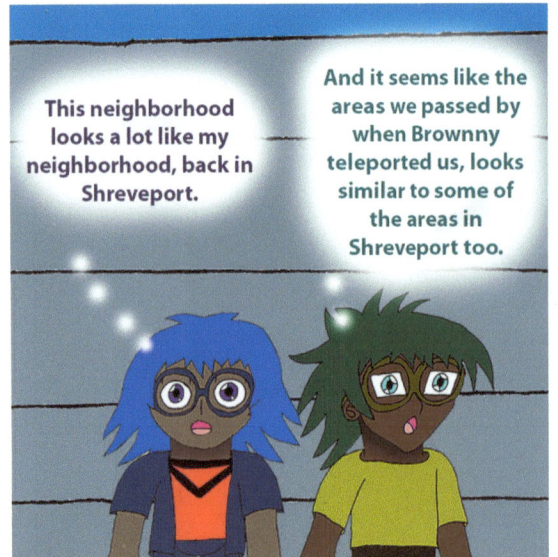
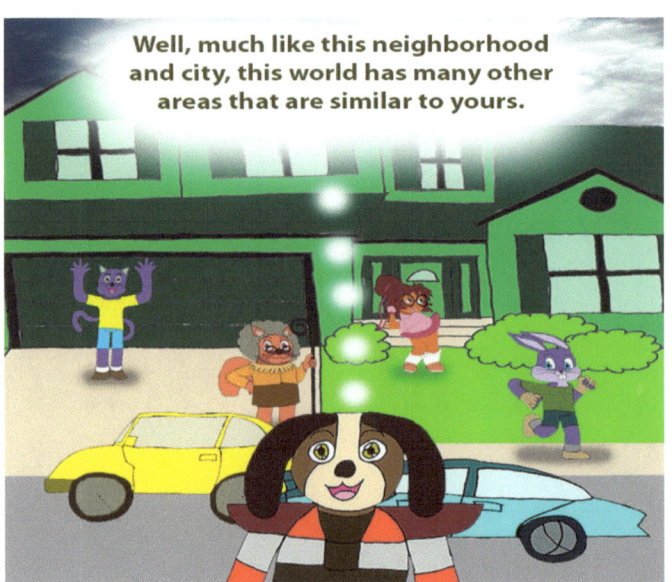

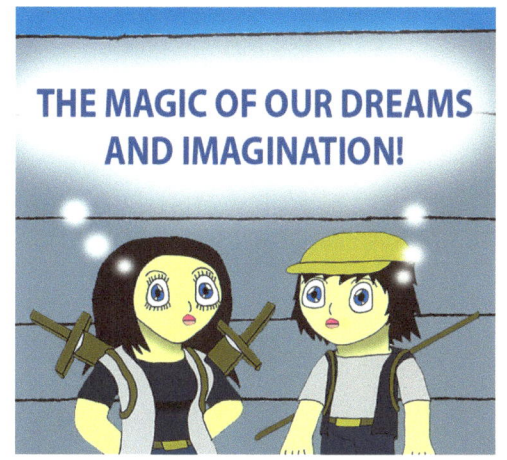
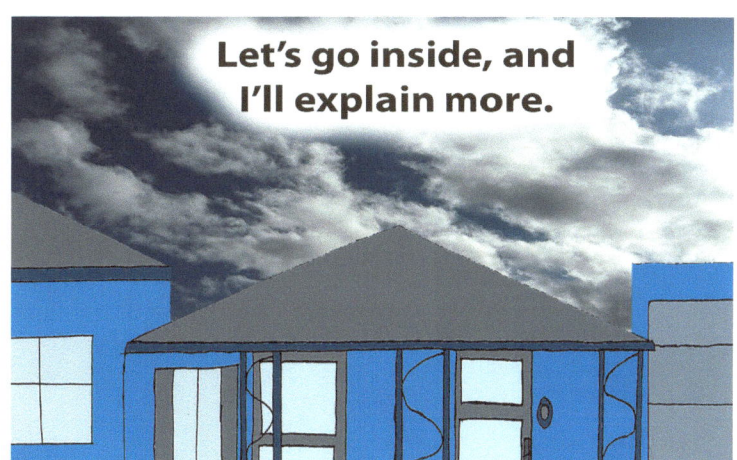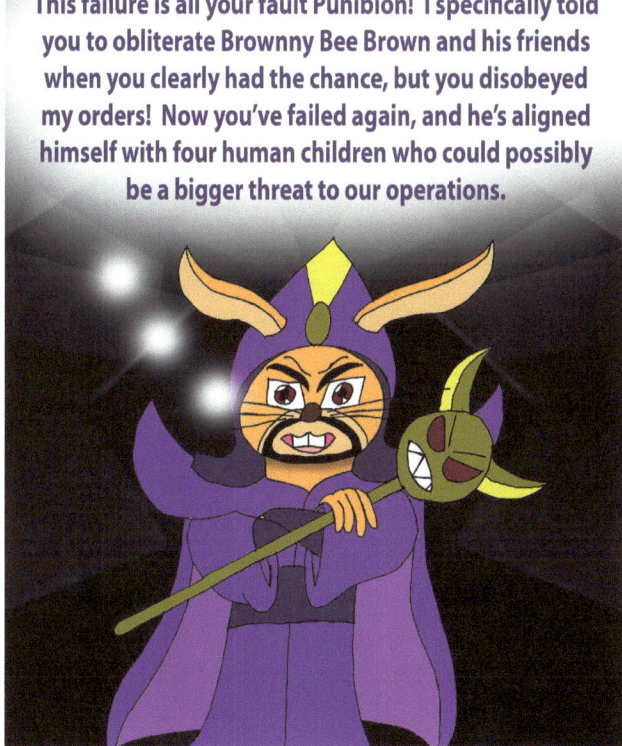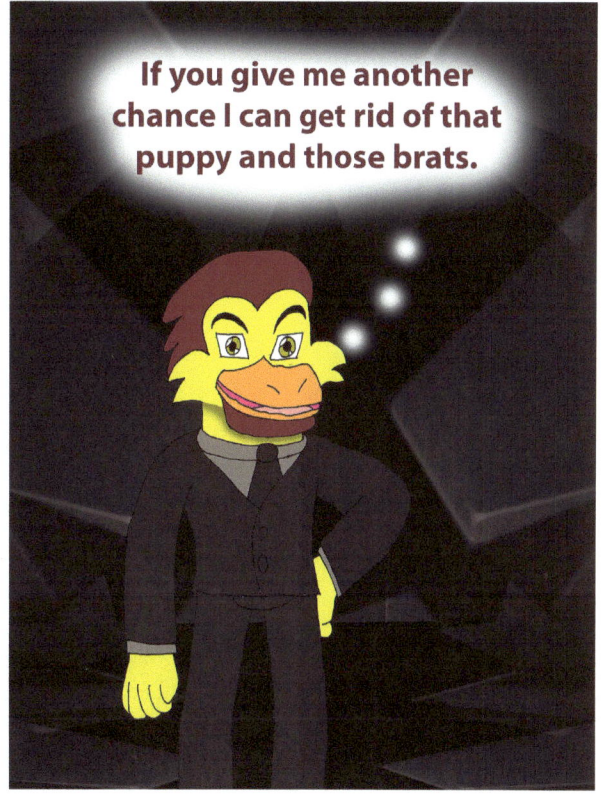

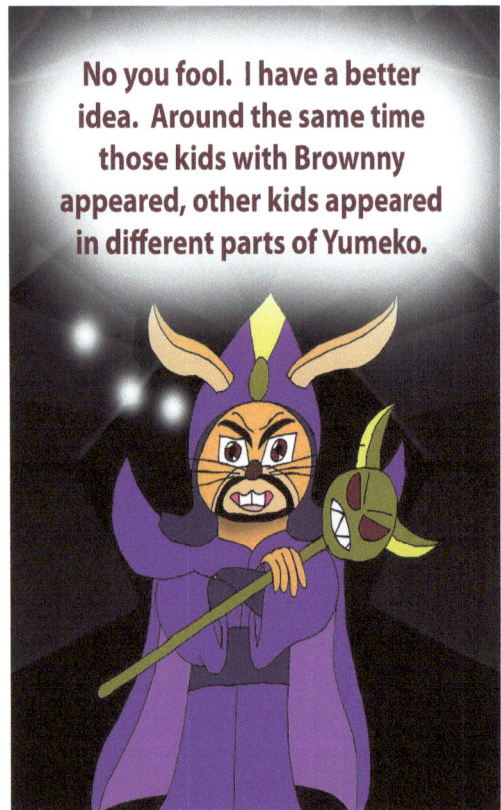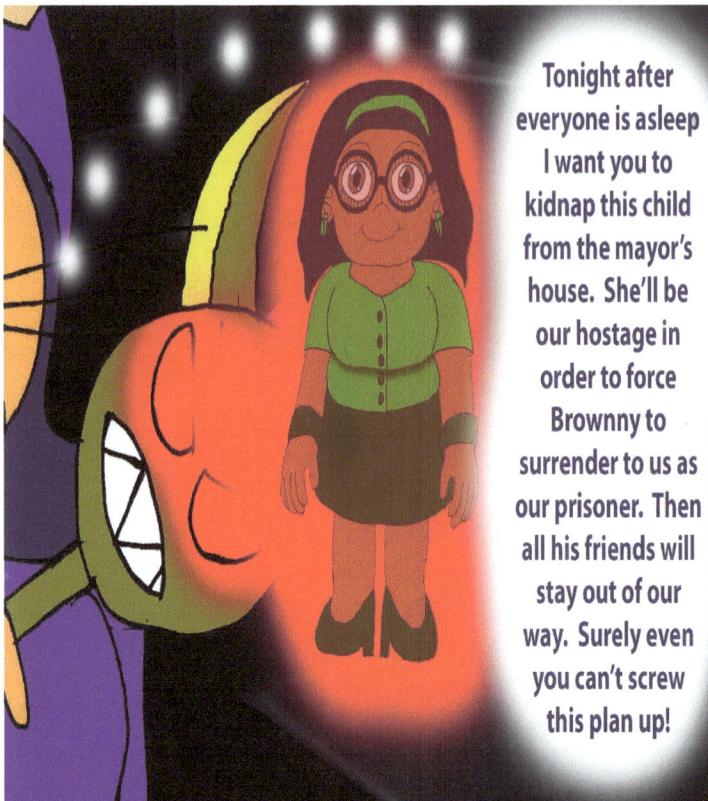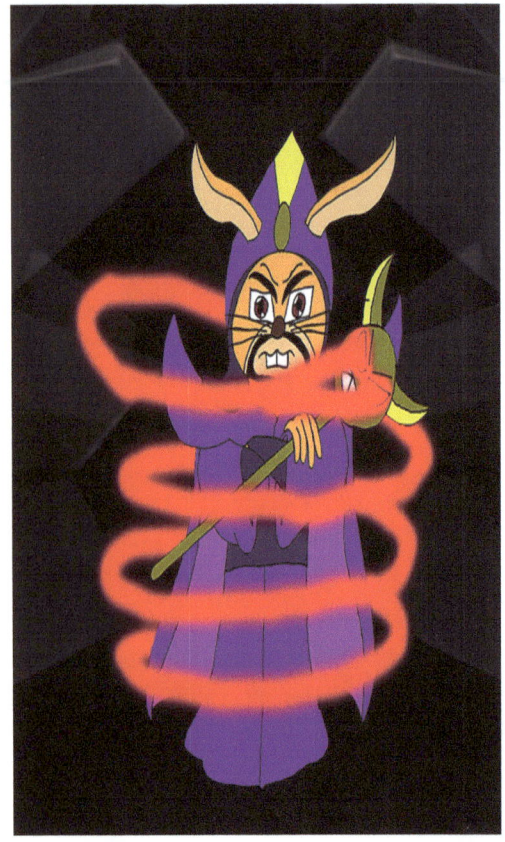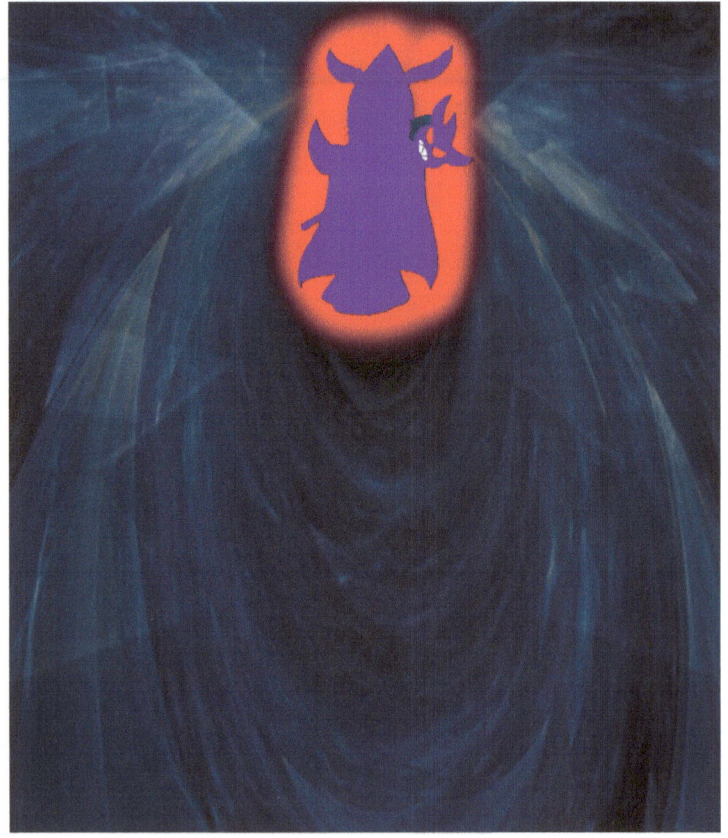

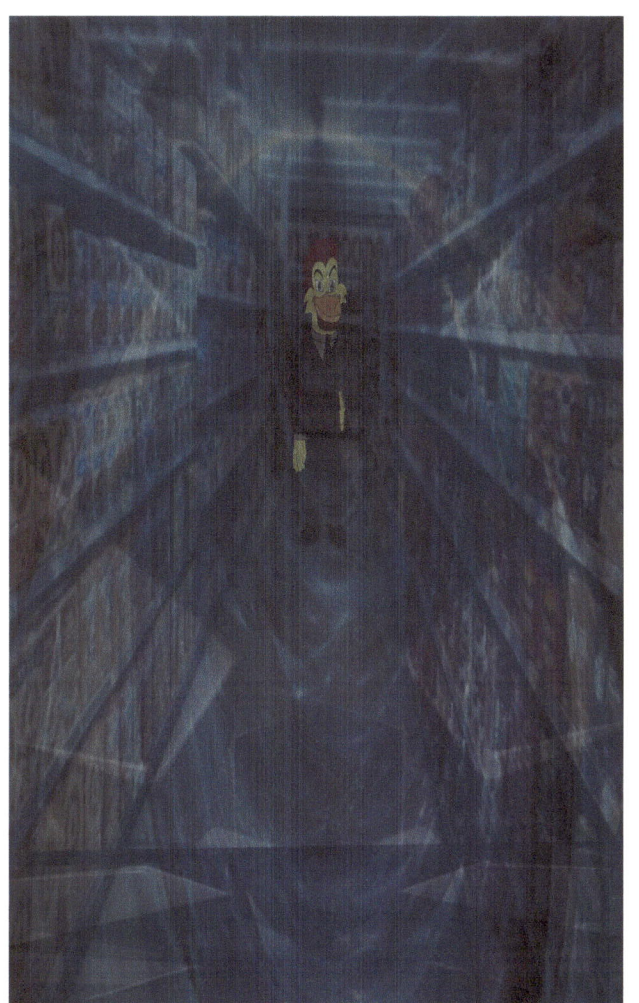
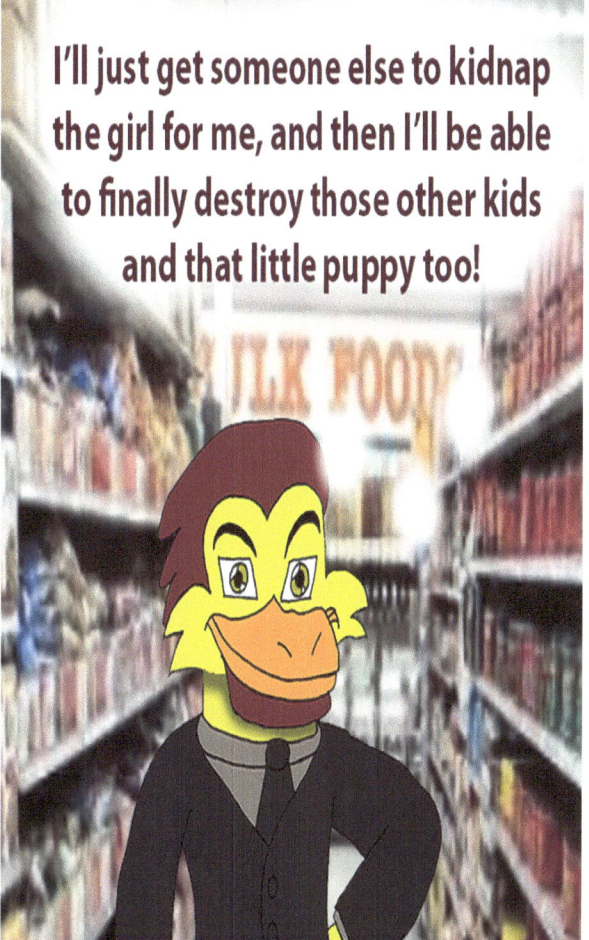

I'll just get someone else to kidnap the girl for me, and then I'll be able to finally destroy those other kids and that little puppy too!

WHOOSH!!!

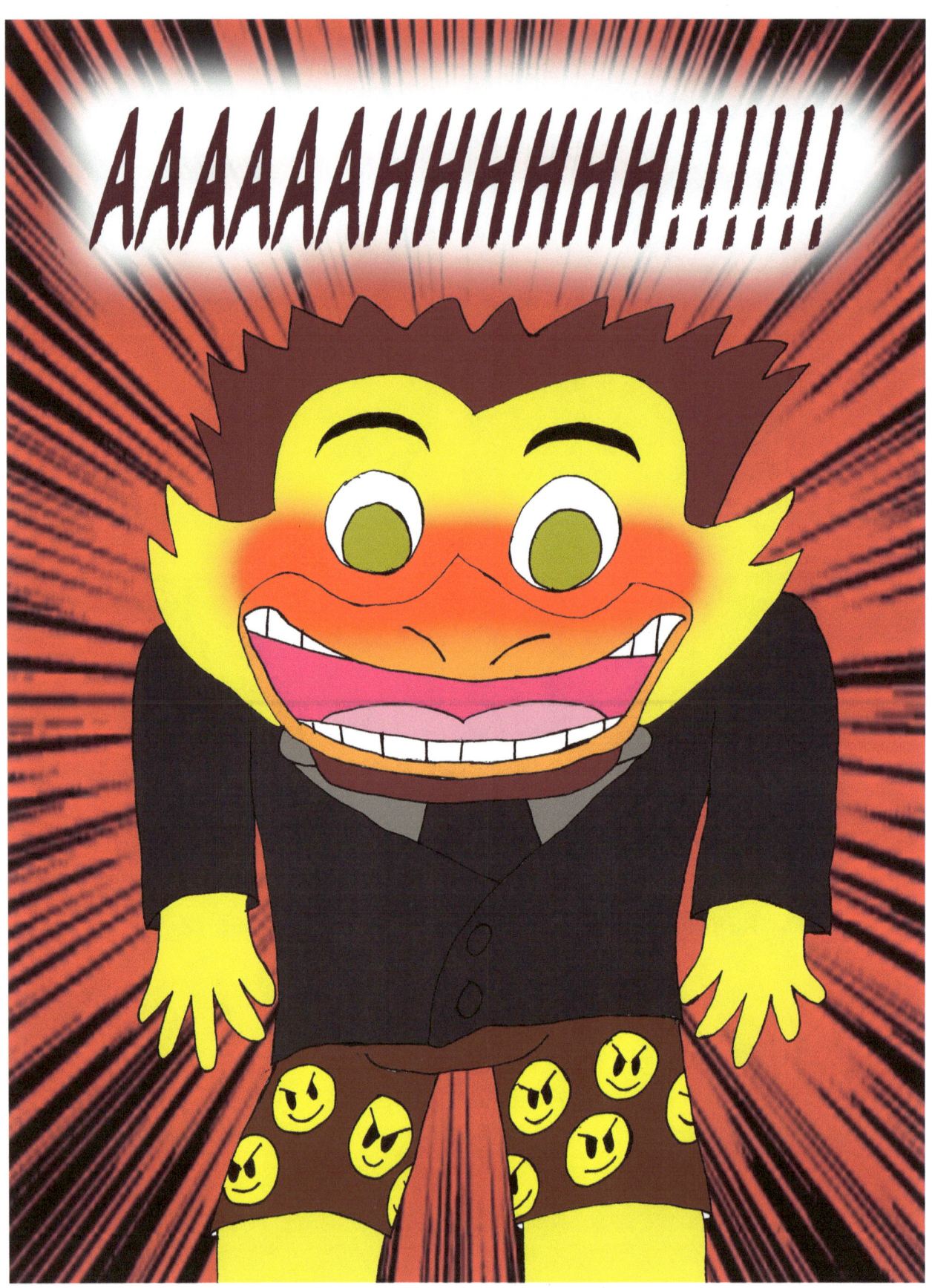

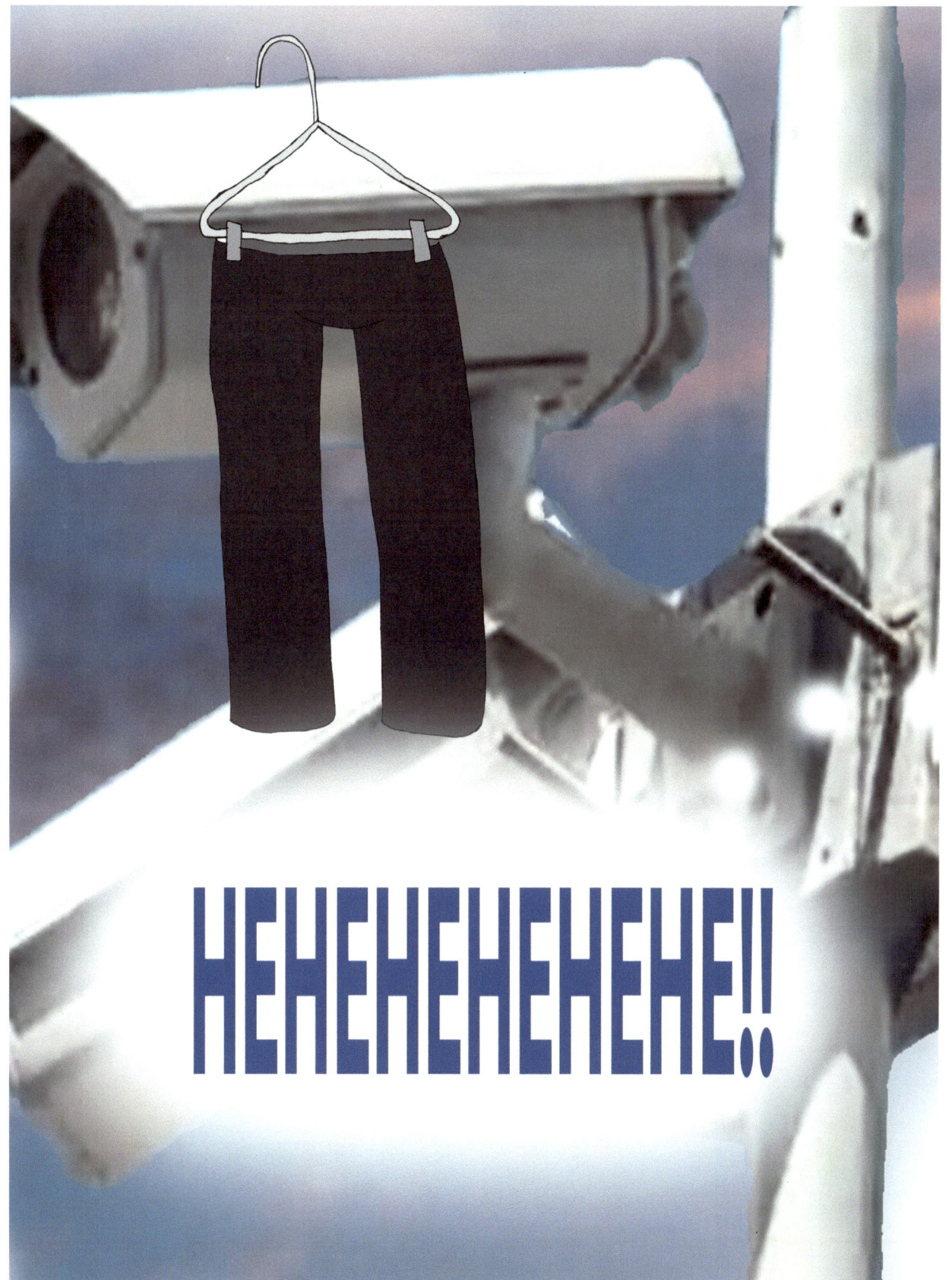

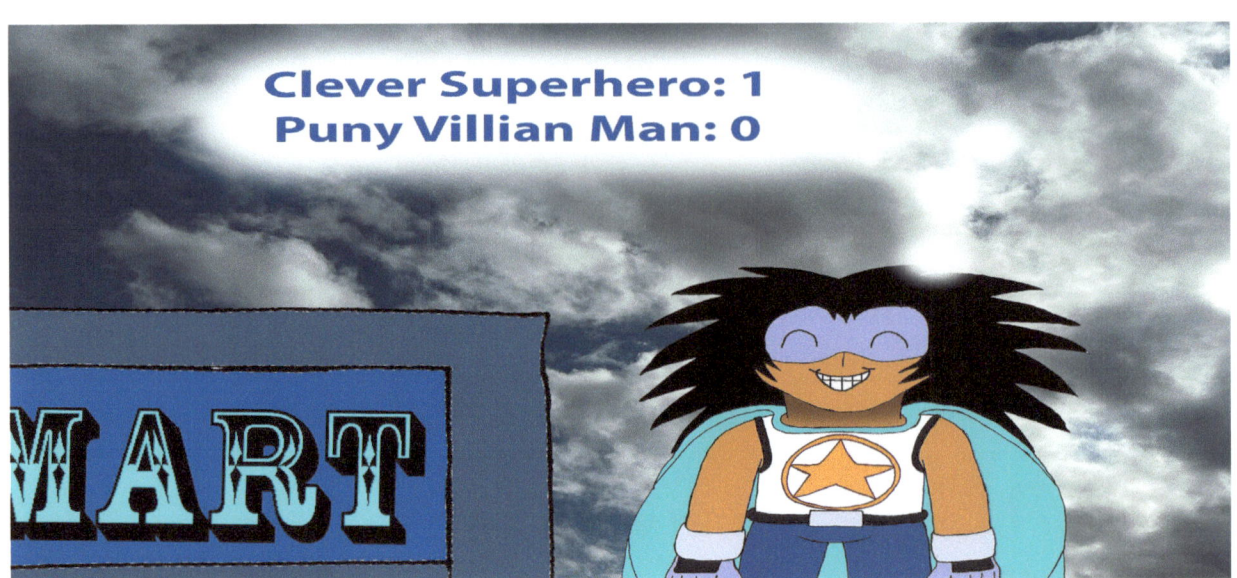

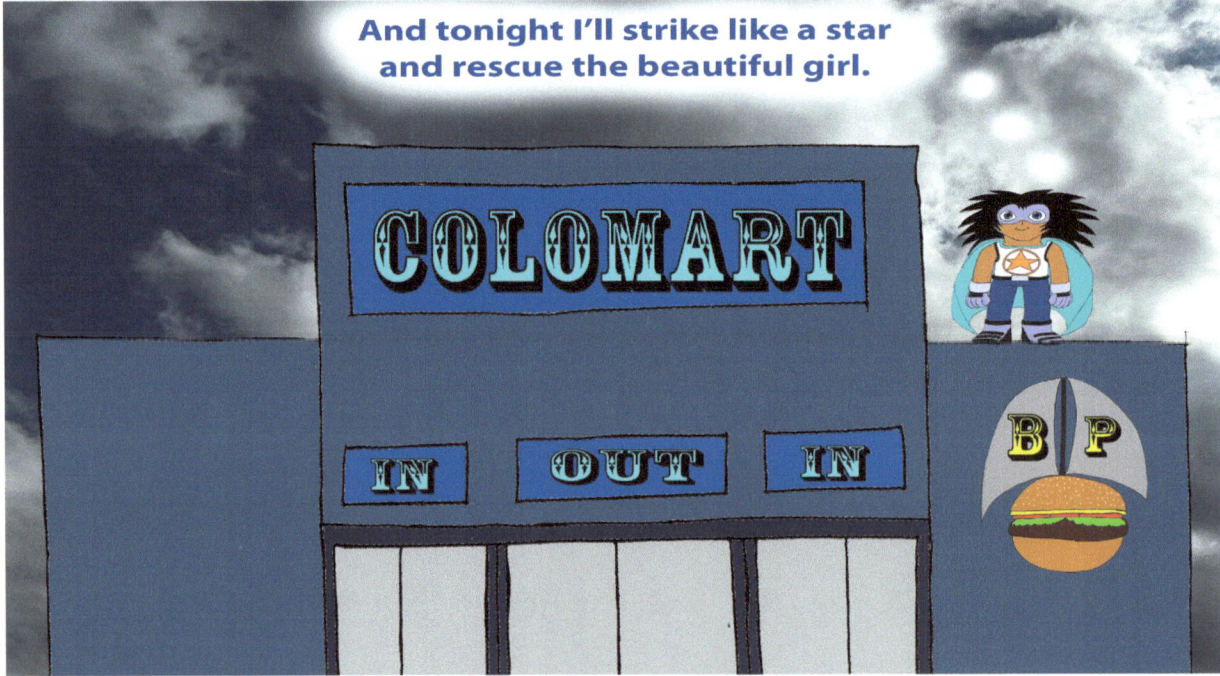

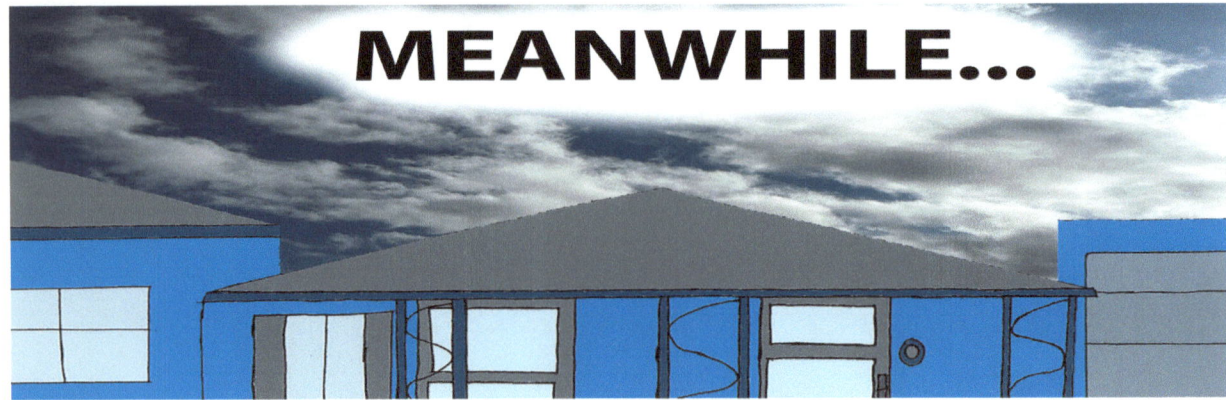

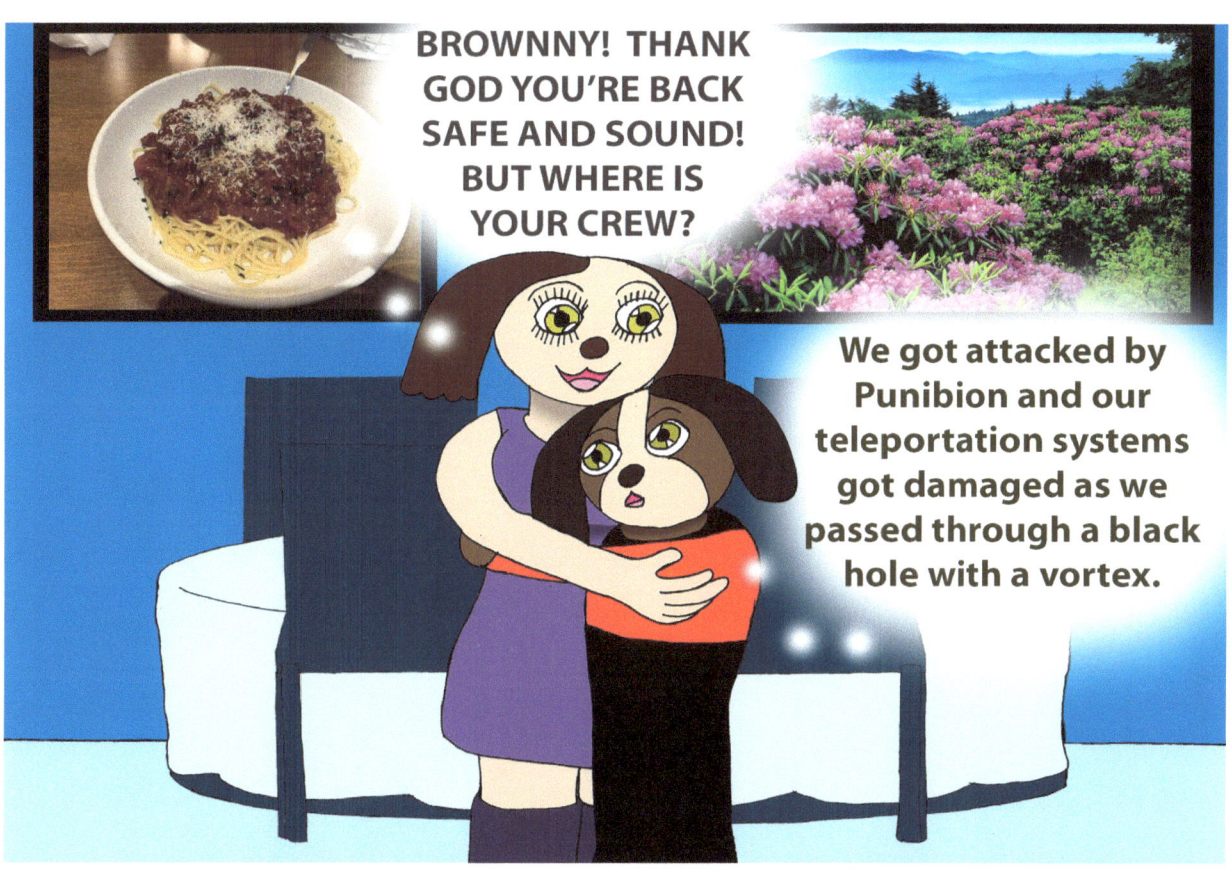
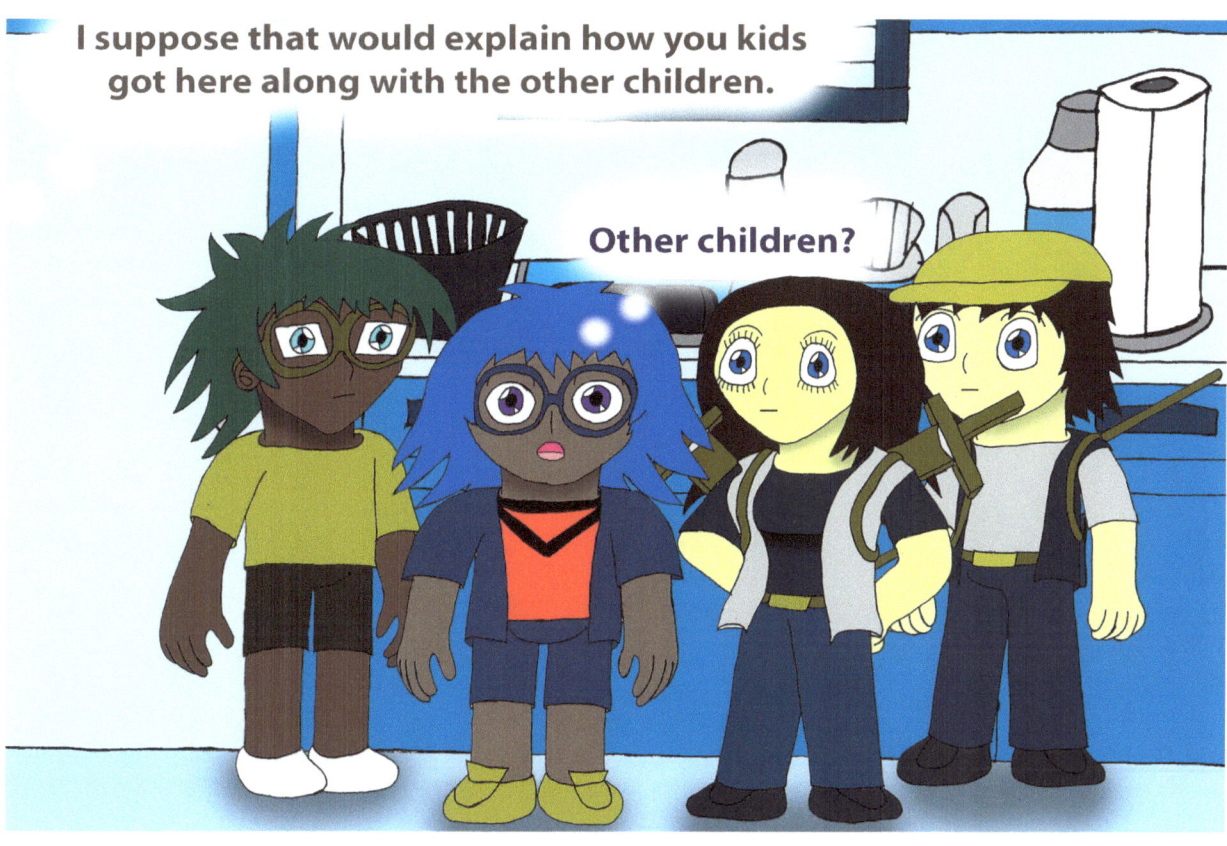

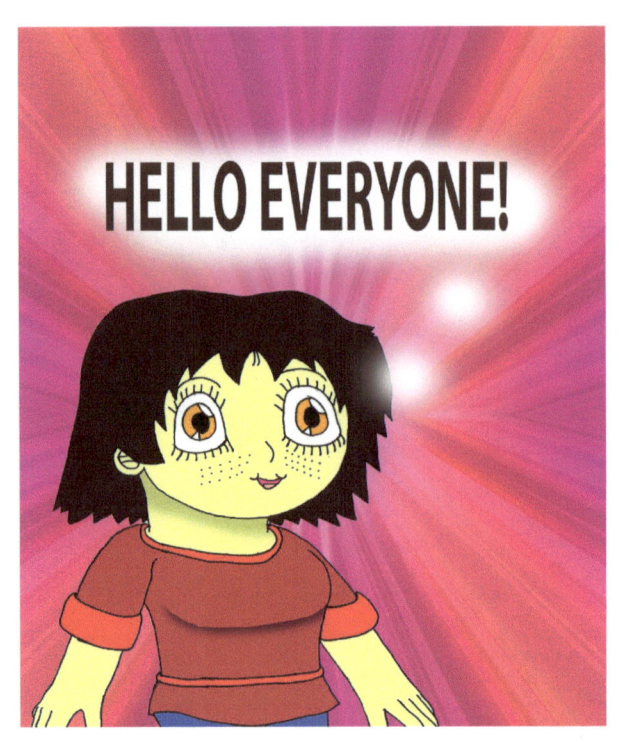
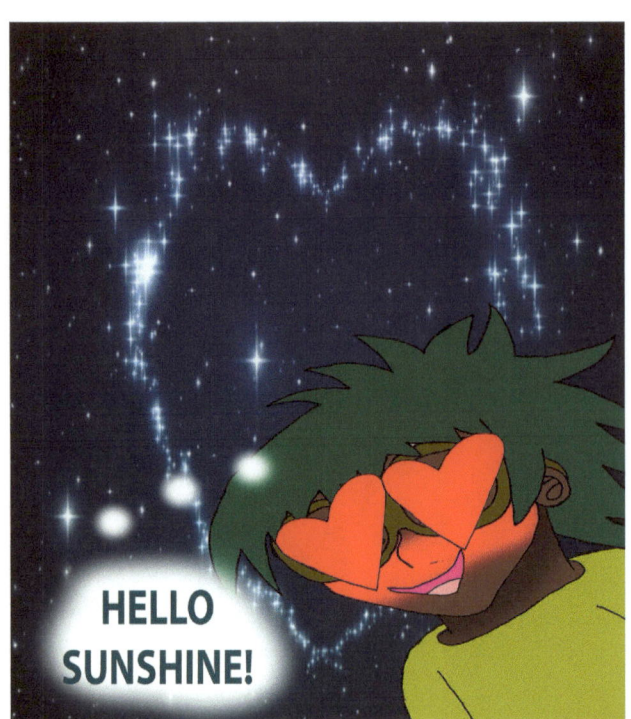
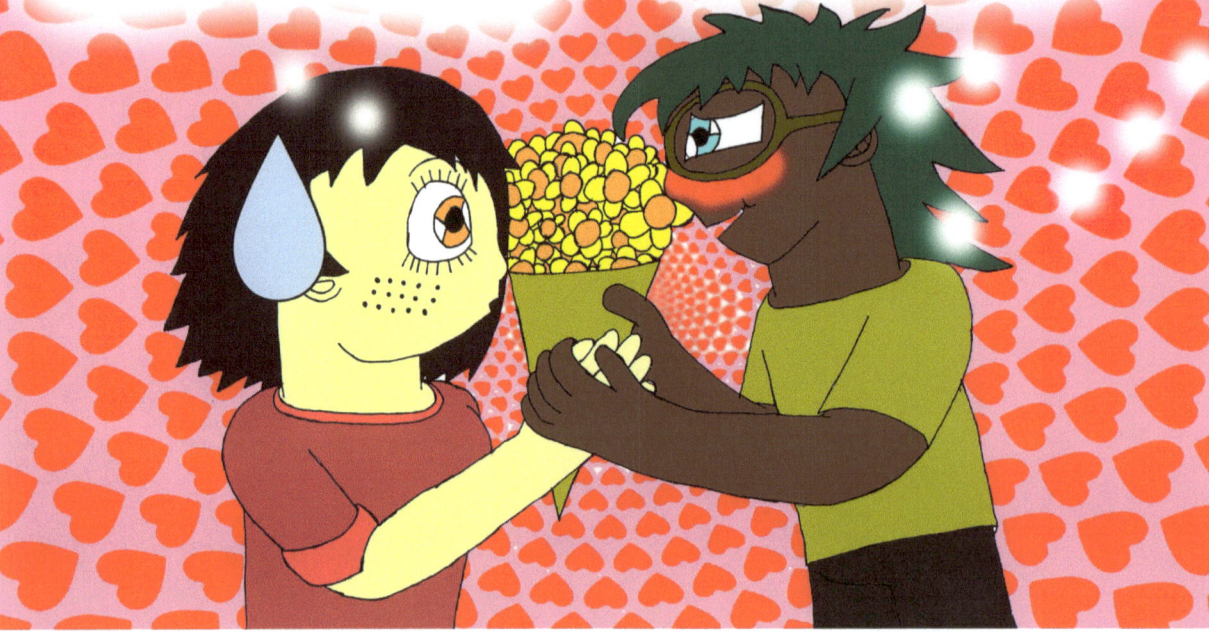

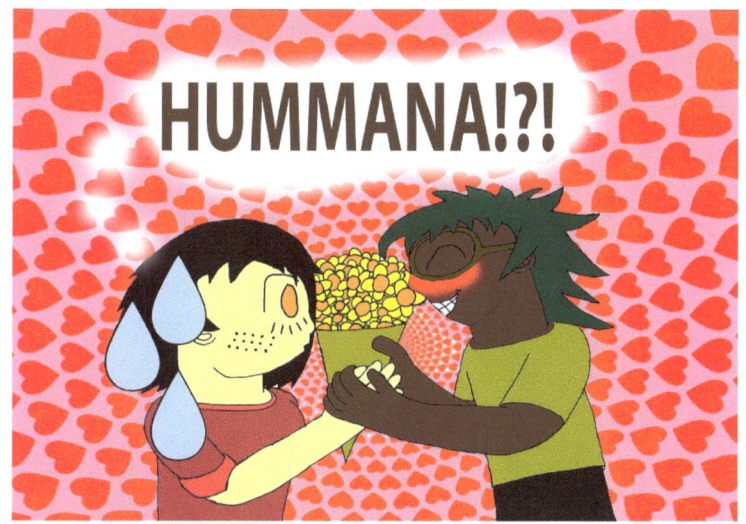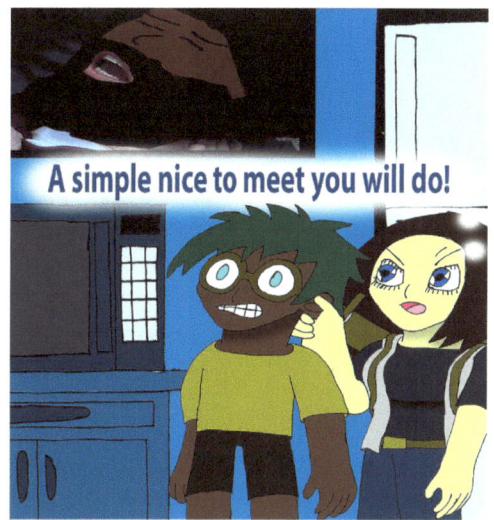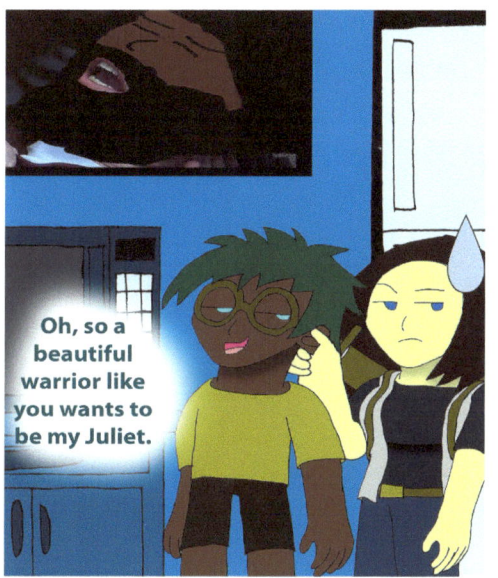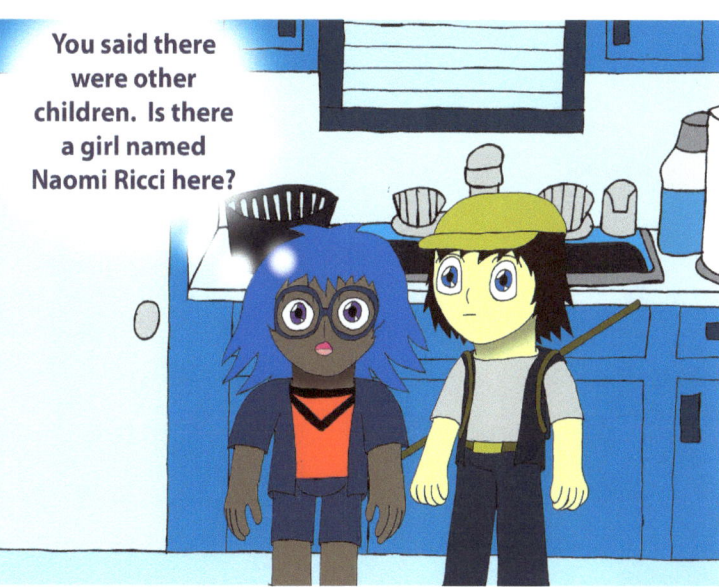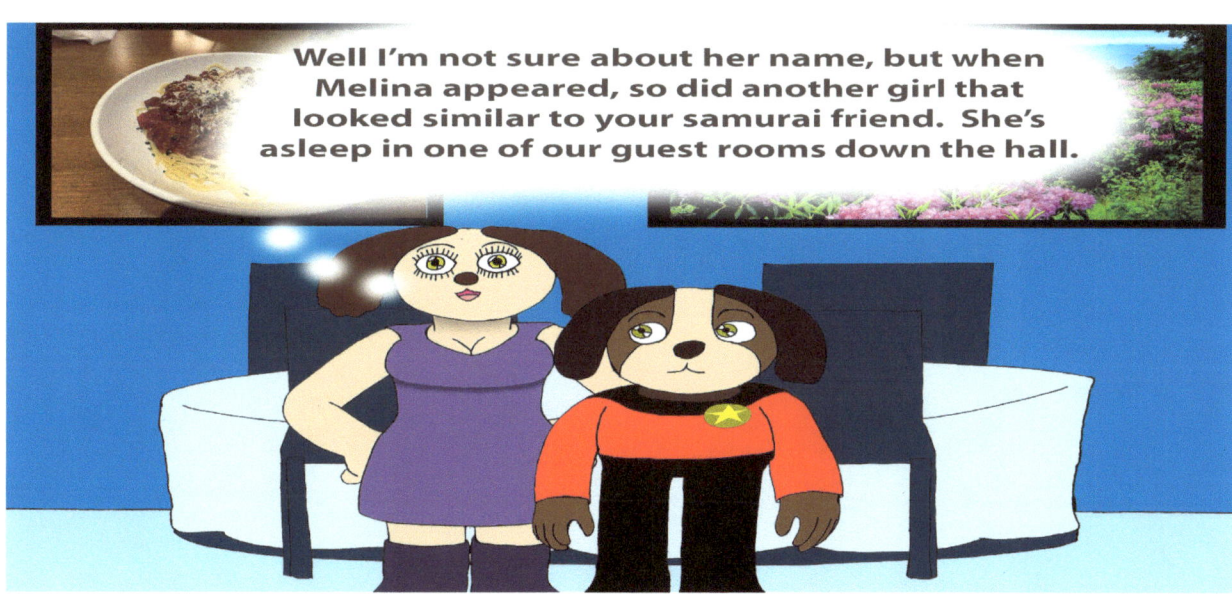

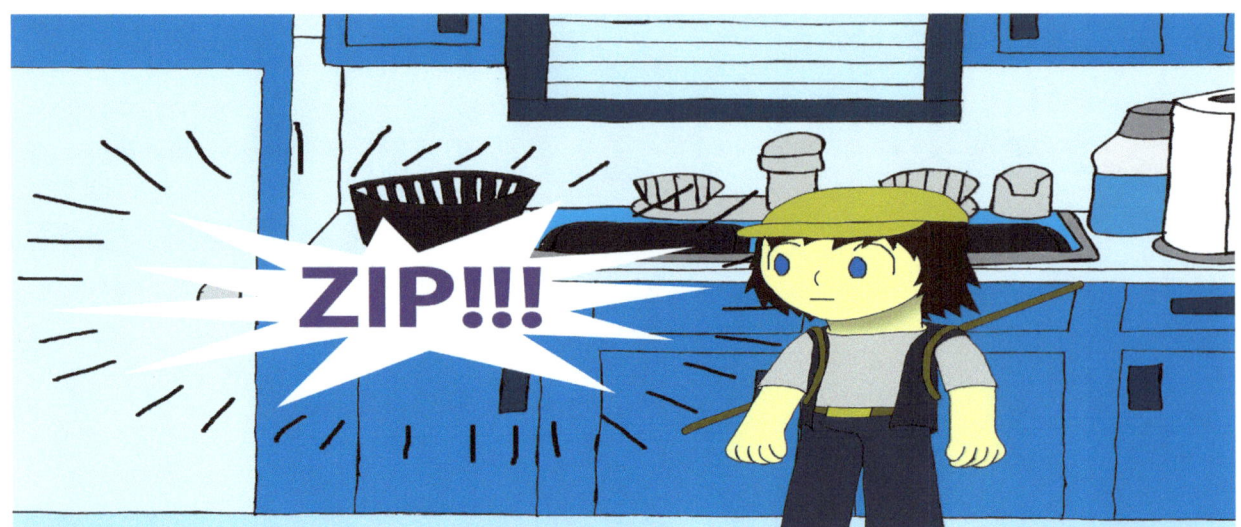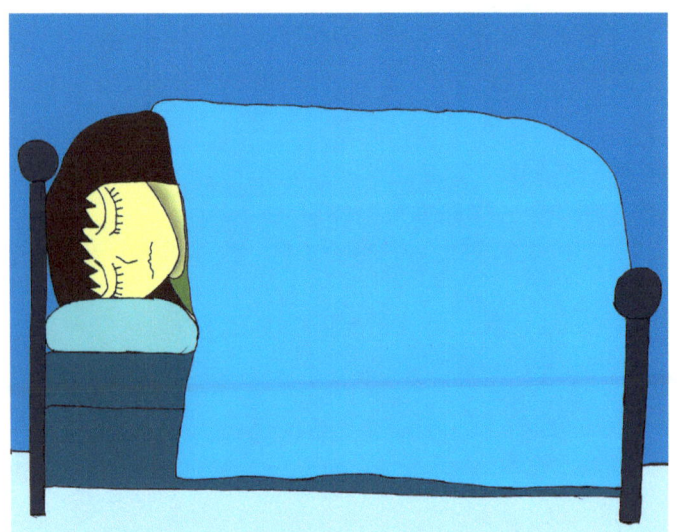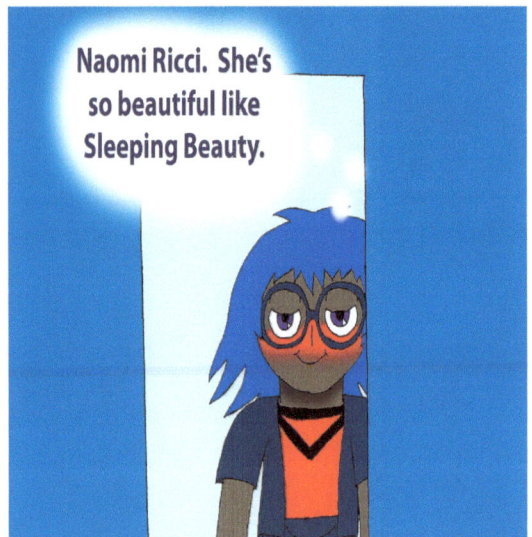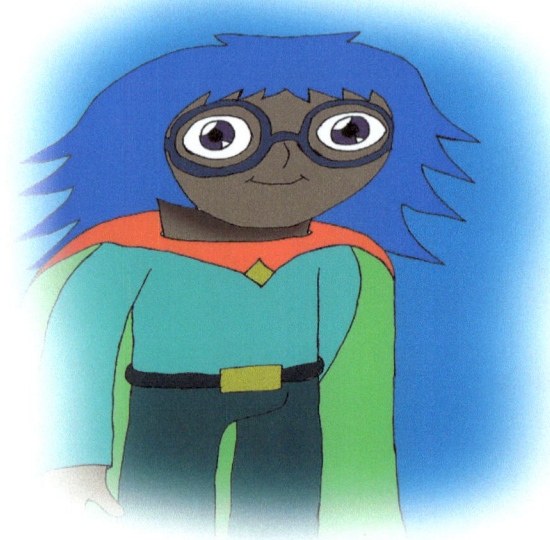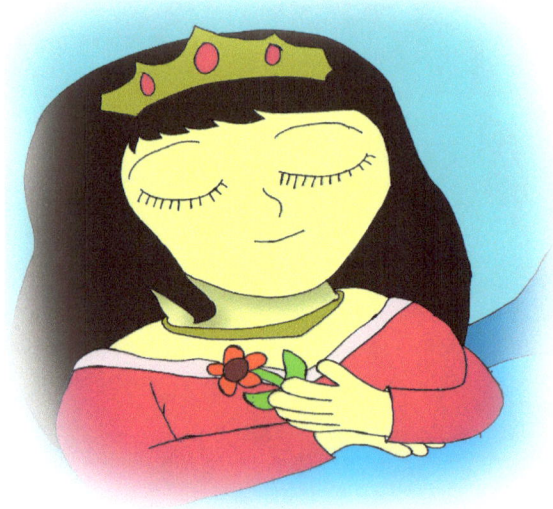

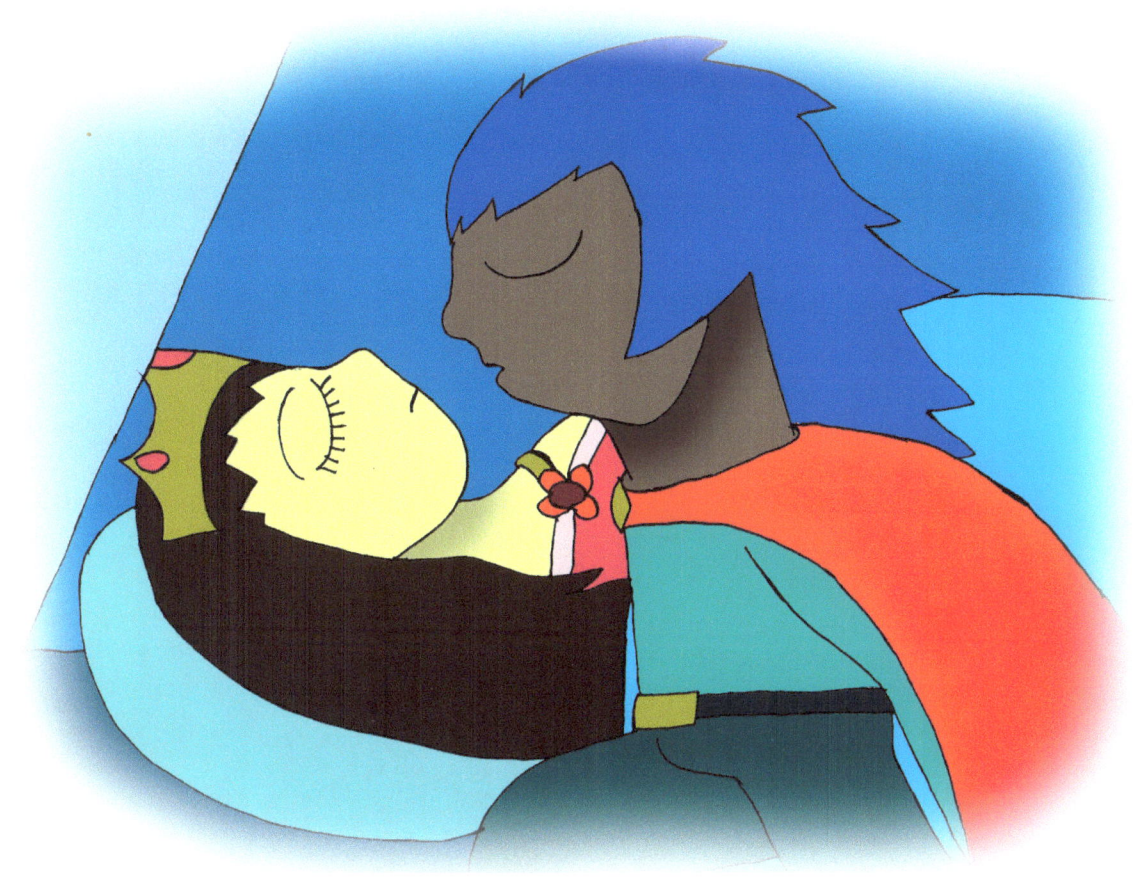
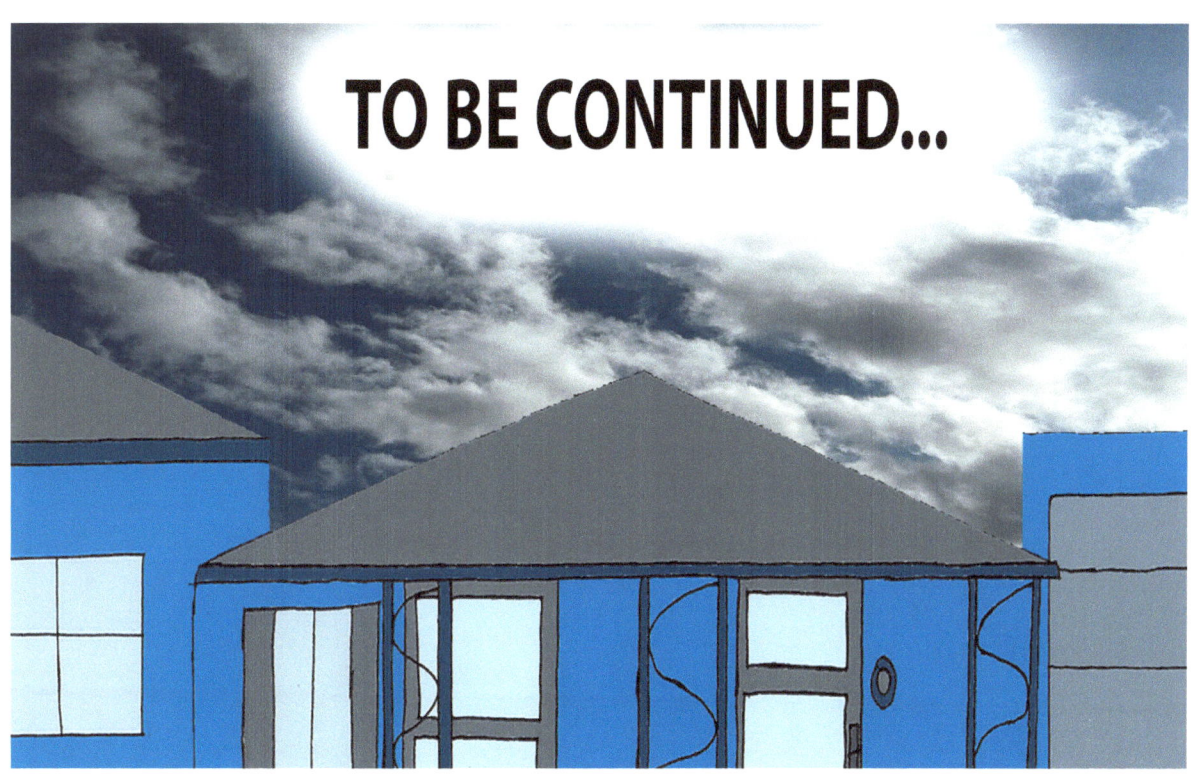

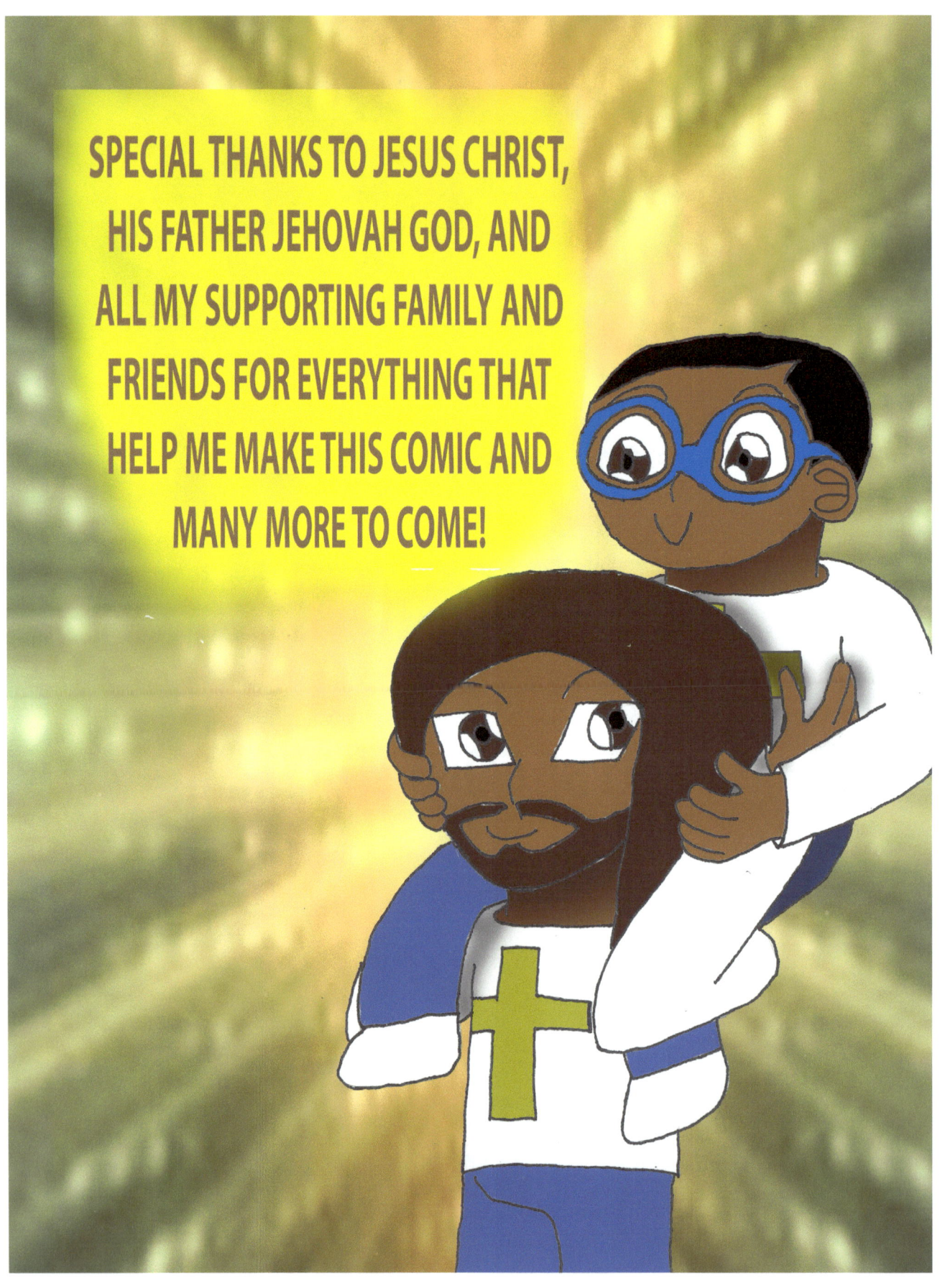

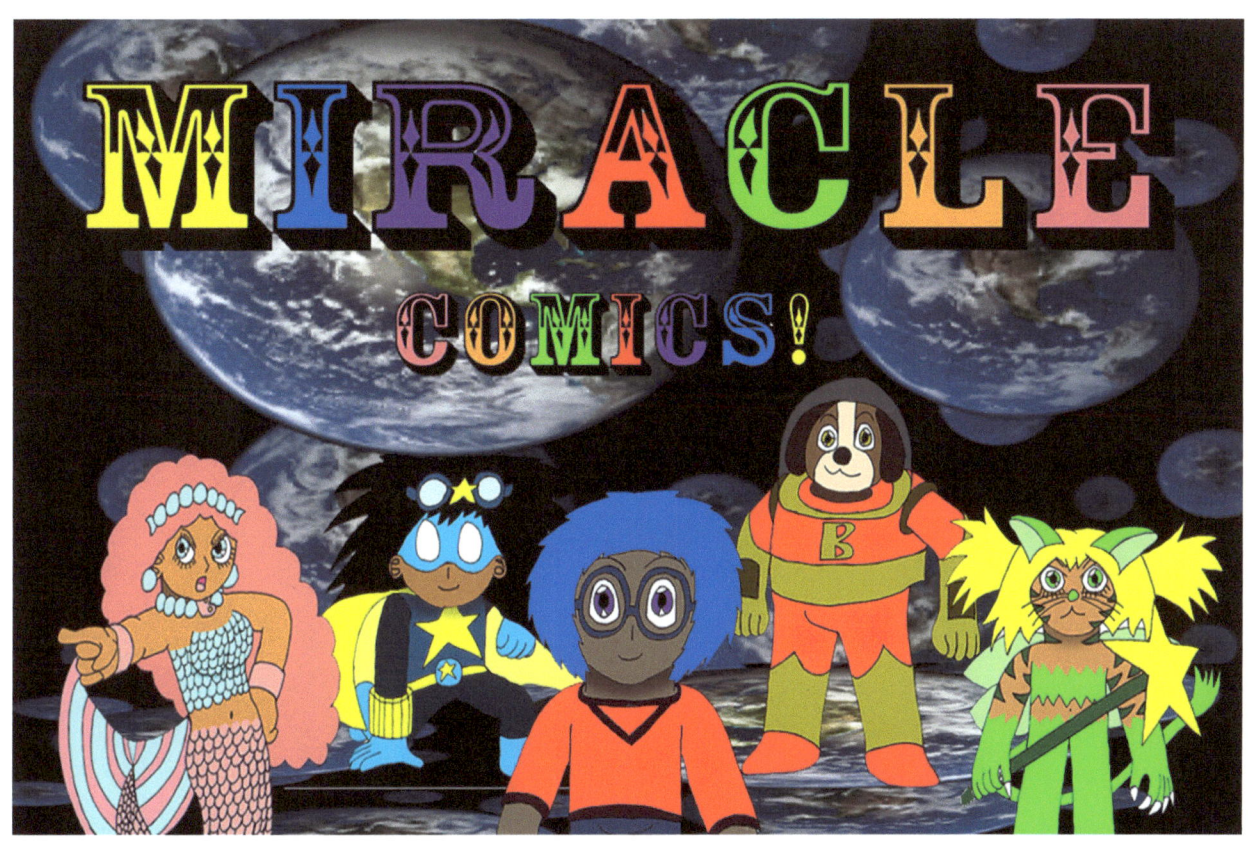

www.ingramcontent.com/pod-product-compliance
Lightning Source LLC
Chambersburg PA
CBHW051831210526
45473CB00005B/1830